Bread and Yeast Cookery

Glynn Christian

Macdonald Guidelines

First published 1978
Macdonald Educational Ltd,
Holywell House, Worship Street,
London EC2A 2EN

ISBN 0 356 06032 2

Made and printed by
Waterlow (Dunstable) Limited

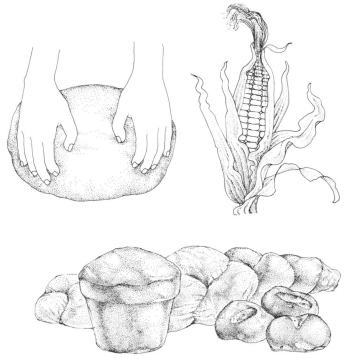

Contents

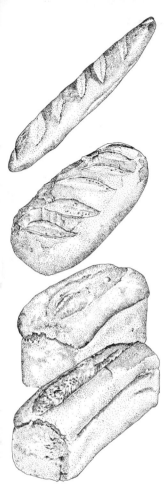

Information
4 The bread of our forefathers
12 An introduction to grain
18 The milling of flour
21 Leavening
24 Bread-making today

Activities
30 Making dough
35 Shaping, decorating and baking
45 Bread without yeast
50 Yeasted breads
61 Pastries and brioches
68 International yeast cookery
81 Sandwiches

Reference
85 Bread in your diet
86 Dough additives and guide to rising times
87 Flour additives
88 Flour composition
89 What went wrong? and cold storage
91 Suppliers and book list
92 Measurements and glossary
94 Index

The bread of our forefathers

There are few symbols as universal or potent as bread—in religion, politics, literature, folklore, domestic life or love. In those cultures in which it is made, bread *is* life. In the secular world it is an accepted collective for all foods and a symbol of domestic welcome; in the sacred world it is blessed with the burden of representing both God's Son and His bounty. Its origins are more mundane.

The early days of bread-making

Early forms of wheat and barley were probably the first plants man cultivated. Nine thousand years ago in Iraq, the builders of the oldest farm known to man planted and reaped grains for the first time; their ancestors had been grinding wild grains for three thousand years already. At that time wheat could not be threshed and 'parching' was the only way to release the grains. After the laborious task of cracking the grain by rubbing or pounding one stone against another, the grains were mixed with water and baked in the sun. The result would have to be eaten hot, for once cold it would be brick hard.

Pictorial evidence of more complicated bread-making comes first to us from Egypt. In the tomb of Ti, dated about 2600 BC, there are pictures of granaries, milling, sifting and baking in pots. The ancient Egyptians are credited with discovering sour-dough leavening and inventing the beehive oven. Setting an all-time precedent, they gave brown bread to the slaves and peasants, reserving the white for the aristocrats. In 2500 BC American Indians in California were gathering acorns to make into a type of bread; Swiss lake-dwellers did the same with a local wheat.

Grinding these early grains was a chore. By about 1000 BC a long sloping stone was used, behind which the slave or housewife squatted, rubbing another stone up and down upon it. It was like washing clothes with a washboard. The development of hand mills with a rotary action was a marginal but final improvement for domestic grinding. Later variations allowed the harnessing of men or animals to larger grinding wheels.

The Graeco-Roman heritage

It was the restlessly empirical Greeks who made bread-making into an art. They added all manner of ingredients, sweet and savoury, and an experienced Greek baker was a worthy prisoner for any Roman legion. These military slave-bakers were responsible for refining the techniques of Rome.

Once milling techniques had also improved so that great quantities of grain could be ground easily, commercial baking became possible. Rome took to it with a vengeance and had one bakehouse for every two thousand citizens; one establishment used 25,000 kg (50,000 lb) of flour a day. By the second century, bread was so important that the Emperor Trajan formed the bakers into a union—albeit one bound to do what it was told, rather than what it wanted. The Romans' enlightened social benificence began with the distribution of grain to the poor; by the fourth century it was bread that was handed out.

▶ This detail of a heavily symbolic painting, 'The Payment' by Lucas Cranach (1472-1553), strongly features bread amongst the expected gold and fruit.

By the colour of his bread

Whether for social, religious or dietary reasons, white bread seems ever to have been something for which no sacrifice was too great. The poor of the Roman Empire, which included the soldiers, ate bread made from the leftovers after grain for the patricians' white bread had been ground. These coarse siftings were re-ground but made a dark, heavy loaf, the carrying and eating of which constituted a major stigma. The early Christians, who seemed self-consciously to seek such blight, included white bread on their list of proscribed affectations, along with false hair, shaven faces and imported wines.

Thus the cachet of eating white bread stems largely from its supposed revelation of the consumer's social status. Wheat was by no means the only source of bread flour: oats, barley, rye and grass seeds, even peas and beans, were commonly used. Throughout Europe rye and other grains were actively encouraged to grow amongst the wheat as an insurance against crop failure; if one died others might survive. But it was only flour made from wheat that produced the desirable white loaf. Only the rich and the Church could afford such refinement.

Bread used in the Mass was the finest and whitest available, encouraging further the belief that white bread was something special—indeed, once consecrated, even magical. After the Reformation in England the religious significance of bread decreased. It had been the custom to mark each piece of bread with a cross to thwart the intentions of the Devil and his hordes. By the time Elizabeth I died, in 1603, crossing one's bread was considered untenably Popish. The cross was retained only for the spiced buns of Easter, when such symbolism was considered acceptable. In Roman Catholic countries today there is scarcely a housewife who will not slash her dough with a cross, possibly without even knowing why she does so.

▼ The bakery at Pompeii. On the right is a line of massive grinders which were turned by slave labour. The great brick oven (left) would have been heated before baking in the same way as domestic bread ovens. A wood fire was burned in the oven, the ashes raked out and the bricks sprinkled with water. An initial high temperature and steamy atmosphere are excellent for baking bread.

A dietary paradox

The working man's lust for white bread has been constantly with us, but in the seventeenth century pressure increased alarmingly. Bread had to be white at any price. Few cared that the price might be that of their own health. White flour is decidedly creamy unless either chemically treated or allowed to mature slowly. By the mid-eighteenth century bakers could no longer spare the time for the latter process so they resorted to the former—adulteration. The most common whitener was alum, which added a harsh, bitter taste. They also mixed in chalk, lime, poisonous white lead, animal bones and, it was charged, bones from the charnel houses. Outraged bakers owned up only to the alum, yet continued to use it until late in the nineteenth century, when it was forbidden by law. The problem was so widely admitted that a famous cookery book published in 1829, *A New System of Domestic Cookery* by 'A Lady', devotes half a page to instructions on how

▲ Basic nineteenth-century necessities: a wood fire burning in the oven, a pail of brewer's yeast, long 'spoons' for filling and emptying the oven and faggots for the next fire.

to discover whiting, chalk, bones, jalap (a purgative Mexican root to counteract the constipating effects of alum!) or ashes in bread.

So it continued. Prophets of intestinal doom proclaimed that wholemeal bread was better for the bowels of *all* social classes. But the men of the fields and factories vowed the bread of their fathers was now far too rough for them to digest. Northern workers held out longer, maintaining a distinct preference for the heavy oat and barley breads that lay longer and more satisfyingly on the stomach.

Only recently have the cudgels wielded

▼ This old Welsh clay oven is typical of the earliest bread ovens, often built into the outside walls of cottages. The hole would have been sealed during baking.

▲ Medieval lords and ladies ate white bread but used squares of wholemeal bread as plates — trenchers. After the meal these sodden platters were distributed to the poor.

Roman Empire, allowed the trades to divide. By 1155 London bakers had formed a guild, which took responsibility for recruiting and training in kneading, firing and baking, and worked to establish fixed prices and wages.

But whoever made the bread, and whatever was in it, it was more than just a staple food. In the East it was your spoon, in Europe it was your plate. Although lords and ladies ate white, wheaten bread, wholemeal flours were baked into trenchers, great squares which were left to dry for four days and then used as platters. Sodden with the gravies, wines and creams of the meal in richer establishments, they were then distributed to the poor, a further association of brown bread with poverty. Incidentally, here are found the origins of the custom of *breaking* bread on your plate rather than biting into it. To bite a large piece of bread was to show disrespect for the poor who would be sharing the remainder.

on behalf of wholemeal bread begun to bruise the preconceptions of society. Yet still, such bread accounts for only a tiny portion of that eaten in the United Kingdom. Now that white flour has its vitamins replaced and we all have much better diets, it probably does not matter so much. Paradoxically, the 'workers' now consume prodigious quantities of factory-made white bread, while the liberated middle and upper classes have given wholemeal bread a new-found snob-appeal.

A self-sufficient dish

Until about AD 1000, milling and baking were in the hands of the same man. Then the advent of the windmill and the re-emergence of the watermill, which had been forgotten since the demise of the

Bread in religious theory and practice

Bread provides an interesting indication of the similarities and differences between Jewish and Christian belief. The Christian religion springs directly from Judaism, which explains why these two religions appear to make more of bread than others. Jewish dietary laws are explicit concerning when leavened and unleavened bread may be eaten. These restrictions date from the exodus of the Israelites from Egypt. The Jews were given so little preparation time they could not leaven their bread before baking it. The Passover commemorates the exodus, and strict Jews will not eat leavened bread during the eight days of the festival.

The Christian rite of bread and wine was introduced into worship by St Paul in

▶ This Greek bread is baked specially for Easter. The red-coloured eggs represent the Resurrection, a symbol as internationally recognized as breaking bread.

AD 55. Though all Christians agree that the bread represents the body of Christ, the matter of what happens during Mass, what effect it has and under what circumstances, has split the Church again and again. The eastern Orthodox Church, for instance, uses leavened bread, while the western Roman Church uses unleavened bread. This is simply because they cannot agree whether the Last Supper, on which the Eucharist is based, took place on the last day of leavened bread or the first day of unleavened bread in the Jewish Passover calendar. Moreover, members of the Orthodox Church dip their bread into the wine, while in the Roman and Protestant rites the two are offered separately.

The Protestants have made the Eucharist the basis of many a schism. Baptists can receive it only from those whom they con-

▼ In Jewish households bread is considered the most important part of the meal. This family is saying Grace before the Sabbath meal, which for Jews is on Friday night.

sider properly baptised, that is those who have openly confessed their beliefs upon reaching adulthood. Lutherans may only participate where the real presence of Christ's blood is acknowledged. And a really strict Anglican cannot receive the Eucharist unless the minister has been ordained by a Bishop.

A food by any other name

Nothing is quite like the thrill of seeing dough rise into a cushion of creamy satin, or, as a countrywoman has described it, 'looking like a milking breast'. Dough has been proven under warm bedclothes by England's invading Normans and by Cape-Dutch trekkers. Sustainer of the highest and the lowest, bread has been served with delicacies to kings, been wrapped around meat and baked into a pocket lunch for ploughmen. It has been flavoured with saffron, with coconut milk, honey, anchovies, oil and wine. It has been hated, wor-

Ο ΑΙΓΝΟC Ο ΜΙCΤΙΚΟC

shipped, consecrated, cursed, hurled, poisoned and used as a base for growing cheese moulds. Yet after thousands of years the basic ingredients are still flour, water, salt, yeast if you like—and some human effort. There is still nothing quite so good as a chunk of bread you have baked yourself.

Bread in the scriptures

Bread's symbolic role has been used in every kind of literature, almost since the written word began. The Old and New Testaments contain many references to it, but bread is not mentioned at all in either the Koran or Mohammed's teachings.

▲ Bread's most important symbolic role in the Western world is to represent the body of Christ. This fifteenth-century painting of the Last Supper by Philip Goul is in the Paleochorio Church in Cyprus.

In Judaism, bread represents the major part of every meal. The benediction of the bread takes precedence over all other food blessings. Full grace after meals is recited only if bread has been taken during the meal.

Perhaps one of the best known biblical sayings is 'Man does not live by bread alone'. The unknown author of *Deuteronomy*, St Matthew, St Luke and Robert Louis Stevenson have all made this observation but each has a different opinion as to what the other supportive elements are.

Palaces stuffed with cakes

The importance of his daily bread to the working man has led to its being used both by and against political figures and commentators through the ages. The earliest recorded political reference outside the Bible is that of Juvenal (AD 60-c.130), who observed that the Romans expressed anxiety over only two matters: their bread and their circuses. In England in the eighteenth century, Edmund Burke, speaking of the attitude of the poor to government assistance, wrote: 'Having looked to the government for bread in the very first scarcity, they will then turn and bite the hand that fed them.'

Marie Antoinette is thought by many to have lost her head because of her fatal remark on the bread shortage. Yet her reaction to the sight of the revolutionary rabble at the palace gates demanding bread ('Qu'ils mangent de la brioche') may not have been as insensitive as contemporary propaganda would have us believe. If the palaces and smart shops were indeed stuffed with cakes and other rich foods, may she not have been suggesting that these should be distributed instead of bread?

To crusading Abraham Lincoln, bread was a powerful symbol of the injustices of the slave system: 'You [the slaves] toil and earn bread, and I eat it.'

Giants of the pen

Amongst the poets and writers of fiction who have used the concept of bread to make a point—or a rhyme—are Shakespeare, Byron, Dylan Thomas, Goethe, Lewis Carroll and Mark Twain (who wrote, in Huckleberry Finn, of consecrated bread floating on the water).

The anonymous authors of nursery rhymes, folklore tales and old songs often made reference to bread. The giant in Jack and the Beanstalk threatens to grind the bones of Englishmen to make his bread— which may sound like a typical piece of nursery nonsense today, but in fact reflects a situation in the 1750s when exactly that was happening in London's mills and bakehouses. In other children's stories, we learn of the king 'who liked a little butter to his bread' and of the prolific Old Woman Who Lived in a Shoe, who threatened naughty children with 'broth without any bread'.

Folklore warns us, correctly, to expect our bread to land butter-side-down and advises us to know on which side it is buttered. The Romans felt it was more important to know the colour of your bread, for thus you could tell your place in society.

A typical English drinking song dismisses bread altogether:

Bring us no brown bread
for it is made with brane (bran)
Nor bring us in white bread
for therein is no gain—
—Best bring us in some ale.

Others would not swap their bread for anything. From the sybaritic East comes the exquisite simplicity of Omar Khayyám's definitive picnic:

Here with a Loaf of Bread beneath
the Bough,
A flask of Wine, a Book of Verse—
and Thou
Beside me singing in the Wilderness...

It is interesting that the Persian poet should have chosen bread over Araby's exotic fruits, sweetmeats and seductively spiced concoctions of lambs' tails and sheep's eyes. If Shakespeare had known these verses, would he have had cause to wonder, in Twelfth Night, whether music is the food of love?

An introduction to grain

Over 90 per cent of the flour consumed in Western Europe, the United States and the countries of the British Commonwealth is made from wheat. It is without doubt, and seems always to have been, the world's most important grain.

Evidence suggests that wheat has been cultivated since about 7000 BC. It is a grass, of the *Triticum* family, the true origins of which have never been determined. For nearly nine thousand years man cultivated wheat the same way, introducing new varieties only rarely. But once the strain known as Turkey red was introduced into North America in the last century, with such bountiful results, the world's wheat farmers have had to change virtually every agricultural, cropping and manufacturing technique to cope with the mammoth crop produced by modern grains.

Now there are said to be over 30,000 varieties, all with their own advantages. Today's crop is estimated to be in excess of 300 million tonnes annually. This harvest is made up, broadly, of only two types of wheat, the so-called strong and soft wheats.

The grains of strong wheat have a relatively high (13-14 per cent) proportion of gluten-producing protein, which is essential for bread-making. When water is added to the flour of such grains, the protein hydrates to form a continuous web of gluten throughout the mixture.

The elastic gluten is expanded by yeast or chemically-produced gas; it is strong enough to trap that gas, causing the mixture to rise. The risen mixture can support both itself and the addition of fruit.

The grain of strong wheat is frequently reddish and always long. It flourishes in hot summers and cold snowy winters, but cannot abide humidity.

Soft wheat grows in more temperate climates. It is lower (7-10 per cent) in protein than strong wheat, high in starch, the latter contributing to the light foamy texture so desirable in cake- and scone-making, when a chemical is used as the leavener. Most plain white flour is a mixture of soft and hard wheat flours, blended to produce an average taste, hence the phrase 'all-purpose' seen on some packets.

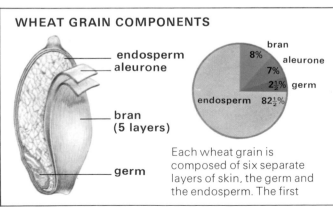

WHEAT GRAIN COMPONENTS

endosperm
aleurone

bran
(5 layers)

germ

bran 8%
aleurone 7%
germ $2\frac{1}{2}$%
endosperm $82\frac{1}{2}$%

Each wheat grain is composed of six separate layers of skin, the germ and the endosperm. The first five layers of skin are the bran, rich in essential minerals. The sixth is the aleurone, which contains protein, fat and more minerals. The germ contains a high percentage of vitamins, sugar, wheat oil, natural phosphates and active enzymes. The endosperm is the starchy component from which white flour is extracted.

The bran, the germ and the endosperm

With minor variations, all wheat is constructed as the cutaway illustration shows, in three basic parts. The outer part, a fibrous container, comprises six layers of skin. This is the bran, only recently recognized as being a mineral-rich food as well as an invaluable source of roughage. The inner of these skins, the aleurone layer, has an additional protein and fat content.

The wheatgerm is the embryo of the wheat plant. As it must sustain the early growth of the grain, it can be likened to the yolk of an egg. Its protein content—25-33 per cent—is similar to that of dried milk or meat. The wheatgerm also contains significant quantities of Vitamin E. Wheatgerm oil quickly turns rancid if storage conditions are not perfect. This is why wholemeal flour is difficult to store in quantity; the

▲ This famous painting ('*Les Cribleuses de Blé*') by Gustave Courbet shows winnowing by hand. This furthers the separation of the grains of wheat from straw, husks and the debris of the fields. The laborious task is still done like this in the world's undeveloped countries.

wheatgerm used in some breakfast cereals is oil-free for the same reason.

The endosperm makes up more than four-fifths of the wheat grain. Mainly starch, it is what goes to make white flour. In its natural state the endosperm, ground into flour, is a creamy colour. With ageing it slowly turns white. It is in pursuit of ever more, even whiter endosperm that man has made such remarkable progress in grain breeding and treatment; but it is in the treatment of such endosperm that some people consider excessive measures have been taken, particularly in the milling process.

Recognizing and using other grains

Barley Hardy and widespread, barley was eaten in China four thousand years ago. It was popular in pharaonic Egypt and Ancient Rome and was important as a bread cereal in Europe right up to the nineteenth century; it would grow where wheat would not at a time when most people were too poor to eat foods that needed to be imported or transported. In Eastern Europe and in Africa it is still a staple cereal.

For modern palates, barley bread is too heavy and moist, but barley flour or grains, used in moderation, add an irresistibly sweet, nutty flavour.

Buckwheat The distinctive, rich and warm flavour of buckwheat has been a staple of Europe and Russia for centuries; the Dutch took it to the New World in the seventeenth century.

Buckwheat is known as saracen wheat in France and Belgium. There, just as in Elizabethan times in England, its flour is used in pancakes. The Scandinavians and Russians also use it this way. Indeed the Russian *blini,* made as an accompaniment to caviare, is perhaps the noblest pancake of all. The North American habit of eating yeasted buckwheat cakes with syrup for breakfast is a direct echo of the breakfast habits of the better-off Elizabethans. Added to bread dough, buckwheat flour is usually very successful—so much so that it is difficult to understand why Western Europeans eat less than one-tenth of the amount they did in the nineteenth century.

Corn In modern English, 'corn' means maize, but it used to be a collective noun for all grains, including wheat, that could be used for bread-making. Corn meal, which is coarser than cornflour, is commonly used for breads. Brought to the attention of the world by the American Indians, it is mainly used for fast, non-yeasted breads but also makes a sweet and delicious addition to wheat bread. It is often sold de-germinated, presumably to extend its shelf life. The intact product is always preferable.

Millet In Europe, millet's main *raison d'être* is to feed caged birds. In North China, much of Africa, and in India and Pakistan, however, millet is the staple grain. From a dietary point of view, it has the advantage of being alkaline rather than, like most other grains, acidic. Its blandness makes it a perfect foil for rich, strong flavours. The whole grains make an interesting

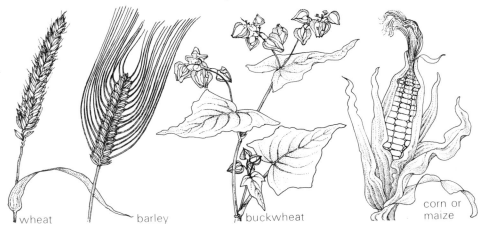

wheat   barley   buckwheat   corn or maize

addition to wheat bread; millet meal can be made in a liquidizer and used instead of grains if preferred.

Oats It is to Scotland that we must look for the origin of the popularity of oats. Oat bread was once common in certain small areas throughout England where wheat would not grow, but is rarely seen today. Sweet tea-cakes made with oat flakes as an addition rather than a base have always been popular, and deservedly so. Being amongst the richest in oil of all grains, oats give bread both greater nutritional value and longer life. It is their oil, of course, which makes them so sustaining in cold weather. Oat flakes can also be used as a topping for bread, either sprinkled in the baking pans before the dough is placed in them or strewn over the baked loaf.

Rice White and brown rice both make excellent additions to, or bases for, yeast cooking. Cooked rice which has been allowed to sour is specially popular in the heavier 'health' breads favoured by followers of vegetarian or grain-based diets. Even the refined tastes of the Victorian lady, however, stretched to lighter rice breads, and Mrs Beeton gives several recipes in her books. Rice flour may be used in bread-

making but produces rather a dry, flat loaf; it is better to use cooked rice.

Rye This is the most important bread grain in Scandinavia and the USSR. A 100-per-cent rye loaf is dense and nutty, for rye does not contain enough gluten to allow a good rise. Usually rye bread is made with about 15 per cent rye flour to 85 per cent wheat flour. Coarsely ground or whole rye grains made wonderful additions to bread. Dark rye bread is coloured with molasses, caramel or, in some modern recipes, with instant coffee powder(!). It is commonly considered that the best rye breads are made by the sour-dough technique.

Soya Although not a grain, the soya bean produces an important flour. China has used it for over 4000 years. It is enormously rich in protein and unsaturated fats but very low in starch. It cannot be used by itself but is one of the best of the bread enrichers. Soy and soya flours differ only in that the beans for the latter have been toasted to enhance the flavour. These flours extend the life of bread and in fried foods, such as doughnuts, help prevent absorption of fat. The recommended proportion in baking is about 50 g (2 oz) full-fat soya flour to 450 g (1 lb) wheat flour.

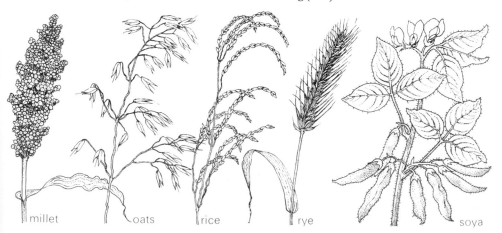

millet   oats   rice   rye   soya

International wheat production and trading

Although harvests vary amazingly, it is generally true that the USSR and USA produce about one-third of the world's wheat. China, for which accurate figures are not available, has been estimated to be the world's third largest producer, with a 1976 crop of 43 million tonnes out of a world total of 416·8 million tonnes. In the same year the USSR produced 99 million and the USA 58·4 million tonnes. The EEC as a whole grew 84·9 million tonnes. Of the 1976 wheat crop, 92·5 million tonnes were exported.

The UK grew 4·7 million tonnes, exported 0·3 million and imported 4·2 million. In fact, the UK is the world's fourth biggest importer of grains and flours after Russia, India and Japan.

Three-quarters of the world crop is autumn-sown and requires a growth period of about 90 days and a minimum temperature of 15·5°C, 60°F for ripening. Newer strains can grow faster and/or in higher temperatures, making them suitable for the otherwise unproductive tropics.

It is interesting to compare 1976 productivity with areas under cultivation. Russia's 97 million tonnes comes from 96·9 million hectares yet France reaps 16·1 million from only 4·2 million hectares, which makes her four times more productive.

WHEAT These are the areas where wheat is grown on a commercial basis.

RYE Rye is grown both for bread and for so-called crisp breads.

TRADE main routes / lesser routes

The milling of flour

The purpose of milling is to break open the grain, thus exposing the endosperm. A liquid may then be mixed in to form a dough or batter. The first attempts at milling crushed the grain rather than grinding it, giving a very coarse meal unavoidably contaminated with grit, stones and other foreign matter. As refinements were made to the basic process of the friction of two stones against each other, crushing became grinding. The domestic hand mills, still in common use today throughout much of the world, were always extremely tiresome and slow to use, and made a centralized grinding system impossible. In Europe, however, the advent of windmills and water-driven mills changed that.

Considering that wind had long since been harnessed to propel boats and ships, it is strange that the water wheel preceded the windmill by over a thousand years. Water-propelled mills have their origins in the time of the ancient Greeks. The Romans used them too, and introduced them to Europe. Historians cannot agree on when the windmill was invented; however, in the tenth and eleventh centuries they were mentioned in Persian manuscripts, and soon afterwards they existed in Europe. It is

▼ The huge granite grinding wheels of the old mills needed constant attention. 'Dressing' the grooves ensured minimum wastage of energy and maximum output of flour.

possible that these were quite independent developments. Both types of mill, wind and water, meant greater freedom of choice for the local people: freedom to grow either more grain than they could grind and eat themselves, or, if they wished, none at all. The miller and his mill were central to any thriving community in the Middle Ages and after; without a mill, progress was impossible.

So it continued right up to the late nineteenth century, which, coincidentally, was when the consistent, compressed baker's yeast was introduced. Then the roller mill, a Hungarian invention, was introduced, and was rapidly and widely adopted. In the United Kingdom, once the first roller mill had started operating in Glasgow in 1872, the old mills were soon put out of business.

Stone-ground flours

The time-honoured system of grinding grains is based on two huge circular stones, usually of granite, and weighing perhaps well over one tonne each. The bottom stone is stationary and the top revolves. Both are corrugated in such a way that the grain is sheared. The top stone may be raised or lowered to control the fineness of the grinding. The movement and corrugations of the stones enable grain fed through a hopper at the eye of the stone to work itself gradually out to the edge, where it escapes through apertures.

The stone-grinding process can produce only 100-per-cent wholemeal flour, and the heat and pressure generated during the operation serve to distribute the vital wheatgerm and its Vitamin E throughout the flour so that they can no longer be separated.

The mixture of components has one slight drawback for the housewife. Parts of the outer layers (the bran) have an adverse effect on the gluten, preventing the flour from giving such a good 'rise' as one with-

out bran. Sifting, or bolting, was introduced to decrease the proportions of bran, i.e. to 'extract' some of it. But no matter how much of the bran is sifted out of stone-ground flour, all the wheatgerm oil and some particles of bran will always be present. For this reason stone-ground flours over a certain extraction rate do not need to be 'fortified'.

Roller milling

Virtually all today's flour is made by roller mills. The major difference between this system and stone-grinding is that stone-grinding is a single operation, whereas roller milling is gradual. First, fluted steel rollers crack open the wheat, the endosperm is sifted out and then both go through

▼ A windmill's operation is simply that of hand-grinding magnified. The main drive wheel **A** is geared (**B**) to turn the top stone **D**. **C** is the hopper; **F** the storage bin The entire building could revolve to maximize use of the prevailing winds.

closer-set rollers. This happens again and again until the endosperm has been purified and sifted into a uniform texture and the wheatgerm and the bran have each been separately extracted.

White flour made this way has none of the vitamin or mineral content of the bran or wheatgerm. Government legislation ensures that some of these missing components are replaced; the vitamins are usually synthetic but nonetheless good for that.

More important vitamins are lost as a result of bleaching. Freshly milled white flour is normally a creamy colour, but will gradually whiten if left to mature for six to nine months; leaving it to mature also improves usefulness in baking. Having thousands of tonnes of flour sitting around is hardly a commercial proposition. So many countries now artificially bleach and mature flours with the aid of various chemicals, some of which are shown in the chart on page 87. Though there is no evidence to show that these additives are harmful, the reverse has by no means been proved. Recently, there has been growing

▲ This Turkish illustration dated 1822 shows a universally common type of hand mill, using two stones and a circular motion.

interest not only in wholemeal flour but in unbleached flours, which some of the smaller companies market.

Extraction flours

A flour labelled '85 per cent' represents 85 per cent of the whole of the wheat; therefore, 15 per cent has been extracted. In an 81-per-cent flour, 19 per cent has been sifted out. These extraction flours are sometimes called 'farmhouse' or 'wheatmeal'.

White flour in the United Kingdom is fortified to contain the same proportions of vitamins and minerals as an 85-per-cent extraction flour.

There is no difference between wholemeal and wholewheat flour. 'Wheatmeal' is a term used for high-extraction flours, but the word is being phased out because it is frequently confused with 'wholemeal' or 'wholewheat'.

Leavening

To 'leaven' means to aerate dough or batter. Gas, created as a by-product of a biological or chemical action, is trapped as bubbles in dough or batter. In the heat of the oven, the gas expands even more; continued heat kills the gas-forming action and hardens the balloons formed by the gas, allowing the baked end-product to retain its risen shape.

The origins of yeast-leavening are unknown. Like so many basic techniques, it may have been discovered by accident. Most early leavening, other than sourdough leavening, was done with ale barm —the froth from the top of fermenting ale or beer. As beer and bread were usually made in the same room, their eventual combination was highly likely. The Gauls and Spaniards used ale barm to leaven dough in the first century.

Today, bread doughs are normally leavened with yeast, or with chemicals such as baking soda or baking powder. Sour-dough leavens and salt-raised breads are far less common than they once were.

Without yeasts we would have neither beer, wine nor bread. Yeasts are an enormous family of minute, single-celled fungi. Each is only about 1/120th of a millimetre (1/3000th of an inch) in diameter, and there are millions of them in the air, almost everywhere. Some are useful, some not. The most important are those that have a special aptitude to convert, by the action of their enzymes, sugar into alcohol and carbon dioxide.

The yeasts on the skins of fruits and vegetables are directly responsible for the fermentation of wines. Yeast for beer-making was grown in a sweet liquid mixed with flour and potatoes, hops or both. A clever brewer's wife would try to use mainly hops with plenty of pollen dust upon them; she may not have known it, but these supported the strongest colonies of the yeasts she wanted.

The barm, which she kept and sold to bakers and housewives, was made and used only within the broadest of guidelines. There was no way of knowing what combination of yeasts had been cultivated or how they would perform in dough. It was this ever-changing broth of many yeasts that necessitated the long risings and provings in former times. Then, in 1850, came German or compressed yeast, made of one yeast only — *Saccharomyces cerevisiac*. At last bakers had their own yeast. It worked quickly and consistently on the maltose (sugar) in flour and permanently

▼ Though they look like lumps of dough, these are actually individual yeast cells, magnified thousands of times; the 'buds' are the start of new cells.

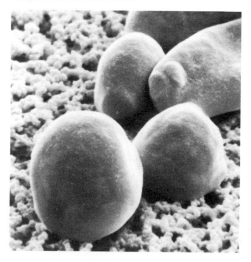

▲ The dramatic change in bulk of leavened dough is wonderfully satisfying to the maker. The top loaf is now floured and ready to be baked.

changed the face of yeast cookery, commercial and domestic.

The new yeast went on the market under three different names: German, compressed and dried. (This has confused many people who have tried baking from old recipes: the chances are that 'dried' yeast means 'compressed' yeast.) Modern compressed yeast is often called fresh yeast. It performs consistently if it is in good condition and can be kept in the refrigerator for weeks or deep-frozen for months (see page 89).

Dried yeast is much more expensive than the compressed yeast but very much more easily obtainable. Dried yeast granules are twice as strong, weight for weight, as fresh yeast, e.g. 15 g ($\frac{1}{2}$ oz) dried yeast equals 25 g (1 oz) fresh yeast. Always use less rather than more dried yeast even if it looks ludicrously little. American recipes usually state the number of packets of yeast required; their packets hold only 7 g ($\frac{1}{4}$ oz) dried yeast, which is the same as 15 g ($\frac{1}{2}$ oz) fresh yeast.

Yeast needs only to come into contact with warm liquid to start reproducing and creating gas and alcohol; dried yeast is helped by the presence of a little sugar. Even under refrigeration, yeast is prone to self-digestion which, naturally, makes it rather less potent than it might be. A clean smell, light colour and a tendency to crumble rather than collapse indicate that the yeast is in good condition.

Magical as yeast seems, it can exceed its usefulness in bread. The action that creates gas is accompanied by other enzymic actions that ripen the flour and enhance the dough's flavour. But after a certain point the bread is said to be over-yeasted and the loaf will look and taste decidedly wrong. Bread yeast dies at a temperature of around 55°C, 130°F. This is a gradual process during baking as the heat penetrates from the crust to the centre. Experience alone will tell you how much rising or proving bread requires in your kitchen; but it is better to under-estimate than over-estimate. The table on page 86 will help you estimate rising times.

Chemical raising

Baking soda is the basis of chemical raising. When mixed with certain acids and subjected to moisture or oven heat, carbon dioxide is given off. The action is limited by the amount of chemicals present, which is why it is important to work fast once the baking soda or baking powder has been incorporated, otherwise the action will be finished before the dough is in the oven.

The need for an acid to start the desired action is why only sour milk or buttermilk, which contains lactic acid, must be used when making soda bread. Sweet milk can be used instead, but if this is done, the baking soda must be replaced with twice the amount of baking powder.

Baking powder is a mixture of bicarbonate of soda and any of cream of tartar, tartaric acid, acid calcium phosphate or acid sodium phosphate. The mixture is bulked out with a starch to keep the ingredients apart and dry. Baking soda and baking powder both destroy thiamin (Vitamin B_1).

Salt-raised breads

Although salt inhibits the growth of yeast, it can be used to leaven bread itself. The method can hardly be called reliable and the smell created is ghastly; the bacterial action responsible for the leavening creates hydrogen and methane. The smell is a sign that the dough is successful and bakes out to produce an acceptable flavour. Salt-raised bread is rather dry, takes a long time to make, does not last long and only works with relatively coarse flour.

Sour-dough breads

Sour-dough is precisely what it says— dough left until it has soured. This souring is caused by the action of acid-forming wild yeasts.

The recipes on page 45 show how to make sour-dough leavens which, once made, can be replenished each time bread is made and can therefore last for months. During the great migrations to the USA at the turn of the century, sour-dough leavens were taken across the Atlantic. Rye breads of Central Europe were traditionally made only with sour-dough.

Most sour-dough leavens include some yeast to help the action, though they can be made with just flour and milk or water.

▼ Soda bread, above all potato bread, is specially linked with Ireland. The labourer on the left holds a partly eaten loaf; the billycan from which he drinks was often used for cooking such bread.

Bread-making today

Bread represents such an emotive part of our heritage that it is always at the mercy of social fashion; at present, much of the western hemisphere has put 'real bread' at the spearhead of the burgeoning movement back to things natural. Stone-grinding of flour is slowly increasing, wholemeal breads have become socially acceptable and interest in baking with wholemeal flours has become widespread. Fashion, rather than Paulian conversion to the good life, is the major reason. In many parts of the world, bread-making is just as it was ten, one hundred or one thousand years ago.

Hand-mixed, hand-shaped breads

In the villages and towns and even the cities of India, Pakistan and Bangla Desh, the chapati and its relatives, leavened and unleavened, are hand-shaped and baked over open fires. The slapping sound of the dough being shaped between the women's palms is a part of everyday life. Some families may buy the coarse chapati flour, but most grind their own as they need it. Similar breads, baked on griddles, are also found to the north, in Afghanistan for instance, although here they are rolled and baked as much as a metre or more in diameter. Smaller, thinner versions of this chapati-type bread are made in Armenia, and the Sardinians still make 'paper bread' in the mountains.

Tortilla, the staple bread of the Mexicans,

▼ It takes a lifetime of experience to be able to slap a chapati into shape as this Indian woman is doing. However, good results can be obtained by using a rolling pin.

is also shaped by hand and cooked on a griddle. The corn to make this meal is treated with a solution of lime in water. Called *masa harina*, this special flour is marketed, like so much Mexican or Texan-Mexican food, by one of the US giants. Few Mexican villagers can afford to buy it; those who can probably have servants to make their tortillas.

The central bakery

In the lands of Islam, including those of North Africa, yeast has long played a part in bread- and pastry-making. The most common types of bread are flattish discs, often spiced, and the oval envelopes known widely as 'pitta' ('balady' in Egypt). This bread has also become the national bread of Israel and is well known to Europeans through Greek holidays and through the many doner-kebab houses that have sprung up in larger cities. Eaten fresh and warm,

▲ In the Arab world, much bread is still made at home but baked by a central bakery. This bread-seller, in Cairo, probably sells his hot bread as he walks the streets.

pitta—whether Israeli, Greek, Arabic, or made in central London—is delicious.

In the same countries of the eastern and southern Mediterranean, it is still possible to see leavened dough being carried through the streets of a bazaar to be baked at a central bakery. Each family identifies its loaves with its own mark. This tradition of central baking also existed in Europe right up to the turn of the century.

The simple life

Countries with a traditional high regard for their food forbid their flour to be tampered with by either omission or addition. This is certainly true of France. That is partly why the French bake and enjoy such good

breads; there is also a relative absence of large baking combines in France: the village baker still reigns supreme. Elsewhere the story is rather different.

The advances of the last hundred years have changed bread-making in parts of the western hemisphere more than during the previous 3000-4000 years. Reliable yeasts, better and cheaper wheat flour and ovens with controllable temperatures were each remarkable enough to have caused a revolution when introduced, from which recovery is still a long way off. The exploration of the freedoms given has given us both advantages and disadvantages. Among both experts and amateurs, controversy over the artificial bleaching and maturing of flour rages. Rules vary from country to country about how much of what should be put back into flour.

▲ On the tiny volcanic Greek island of Santorini the first winnowing of the wheat is still done in the fields with pitchforks and a convenient breeze.

The sliced-loaf phenomenon

Roller milling has its supporters and its fanatical opponents. In pursuit of more output for less manpower, man has created the continuous bread-making process and introduced bread aerated by chemical means, neither of which can result in any approximation of true bread flavour, whatever the flour used.

The financially-based delight with which these bread-making innovations were greeted has now died, and during the 'sixties several countries quietly dropped the methods and went back to older batch-baking methods. Chemically aerated bread, other than soda bread, is no longer made commercially.

The phenomenon of the modern, chemically-assisted, fast-rising, sliced white loaf that is marketed mainly in the USA, the Netherlands, the UK and parts of the British Commonwealth, is currently controversial. Essentially, the dough for this product is mixed, risen and being baked within the hour. The end-product smells right, slices like a dream, does not crumble when spread with butter and jam and keeps well. And that, claim the manufacturers, is what is expected of bread. The flavour seems not to matter: according to the manufacturers, as long as people buy the bread, the flavour must be what they want.

The truth is that in the UK at least, commercial bread-baking is controlled by just a few huge combines who also spend millions of pounds on advertising. With their competitive pricing and massive advertising they have forced many small bakers out of business, leaving the consumer no choice other than an alternative brand of the same chemical mass.

To be fair, this type of bread is probably just as good for you as other breads, although the full effects of some of the additives are still not known. The voices of protest have seeped through to the boardrooms, however, and now there is a torrent of new health loaves from the combines containing bran and goodness knows what else. Recently, too, there has been the advent of the High Street 'hot bread shop'. And that is possibly the unkindest uncut loaf of all.

The quest for real bread

Asked what was the nicest thing about baking bread, most people would put 'the smell' quite high on their list. The smell is exactly what the new 'crusty-bread-baked-on-the-premises' shops are selling—the wonderful aroma of bread that spells home, hearth and comfort even to those who have never kneaded, proved or plaited.

But it is a confidence trick: all those breads are made with the fast chemical doughs, and are given barely enough time to breathe, let alone mature. In fact, yeasted bread, no matter how ghastly, always smells divine while baking. Stripped-pine decor, wrought iron, bricks and brown paper bags are just part of the carefully thought-out strategy of selling that smell to re-kindle interest in a market for mass-produced bread that is gradually dying.

▼ Of all the extraordinary things you can do with bread, this must be the most astonishing—a chandelier of bread in a French shop devoted entirely to bread and dough.

bread. In a bread strike in Britain during late 1977, the giant baking companies lost ten per cent of their business, permanently. Then, early in 1978, one went out of business, revealing losses of £28 million over six years. Being forced to eat other breads, or to discover how easy bread is to bake at home, made thousands of customers eschew the chemical product they thought was irreplaceable, forever. It is a lesson worth learning, without waiting for a bread strike to occur. For whatever you decide to believe about the relative merits of wholemeal and white flours, homemade breads are incontrovertibly more delicious, more satisfying and more interesting.

▶ Crusty bloomers, farmhouse and tin loaves like this are made by the big baking combines but use dough that is made in new ways: the gluten is stretched by high-speed beating rather than the gentle action of yeast. Only public pressure will ensure that real bread continues to be available.

▲ The true French *baguette* is stale in just a few hours, so bakers like this one in Paris make fresh batches every few hours and sell them as soon as possible. The short life stems from the use of soft flour which absorbs little moisture.

It would be unjust to dismiss all mass-production of bread; to do so would be to injure thousands of small businesses around the world. Right in the centre of New York, London, Sydney and, no doubt, Rio de Janeiro, you will find small businesses baking in bulk, certainly, but doing so with respect for tradition and their customers. Just behind Harrods store in London's Knightsbridge, a 150-year-old brick oven is daily fired with wood. Only a few kilometres away, a wholefood bakery uses only flour that is specially stone-ground for it daily, again in Greater London. Similar stories can certainly be told elsewhere.

It will take a long time for some countries to make their modern breads more like those that have been replaced, if only because so much money has been invested in the technology of the quick-risen white

▼ At Munich's famous Oktoberfest, beer-drinkers and revellers are confronted by mountains of fanciful pretzels, poppy-seed rolls and traditional German bread shapes.

Making dough

Good yeasted bread needs good dough. Good dough needs good kneading ... that's all there is to it! Choose the dough method you like best, plan your timetable and remember to have everything warm, including the flour and the mixing bowl. Your reward, a cushion of creamy dough, will always repay the effort.

Equipment

The wonderful thing about dough-making is that it does not need any equipment that would not normally be found in a kitchen. A large mixing bowl, a wooden board or laminated surface, some kitchen scales and a measuring jug are the basic requirements. Loaf tins help give more professional-looking results. A room thermometer is useful, and so is one for measuring the temperature of liquids.

Ingredients

Flour White flour for bread-making should be plainly labelled 'strong' or carry some other statement of its suitability for bread-making. Never use self-raising flour. It is unwise to buy large amounts of wholemeal flour, because the fat it contains can go rancid; the flour also tends to attract insects.

Yeast This is most commonly available in dried, granulated form. If you are used to using fresh yeast, do not be alarmed at the comparatively small quantities of dried yeast called for in bread recipes. *Don't* be tempted to use more—it is the use of too much dried yeast that has given it a bad name in some circles. Properly used, it should give results that are indistinguishable to all but the most discerning palates.

Salt This is a most important part of bread-making, not just for flavouring but also because it tempers the growth of the yeast, strengthens the gluten and keeps long-rising doughs sweet. Measure salt very carefully. The amount of salt used is a matter of personal taste, but does affect the rising time: the more salt used, the more time will be needed.

Liquid The most common liquid in bread-making is lukewarm water. A softer crumb results if a proportion of milk is used: one-third

milk, two-thirds water is reckoned to be the maximum if the texture is not to become cake-like. The milk should always be scalded — that is, brought just to the boil, then cooled; scalding is especially recommended if you are going to make an all-milk loaf, because it stops the interaction of milk enzymes with the yeast's growth.

Potato water is an excellent dough-mixer. Either use water in which potatoes have been cooked, or grate or mash some cooked potato into its cooking water. **Fat** Butter, margarine, lard and any vegetable oil can be used to improve or alter flavour and texture; they also delay staling. Oil is very easy to incorporate but fat gives a better texture and colour.

Other ingredients These include eggs, molasses, honey, sugar, milk powder and soya flour. In most cases, adaptation of the recipe is required.

Methods

There are two basic methods of making dough for bread. In one, the sponge method, yeast and liquid are mixed with only a portion of the flour and there is no salt to inhibit the yeast. In the other method, described here as 'all-in', all the flour is used right from the start. Correctly carried out, both methods have their advantages.

The sponge method This is the older method, advocated by virtually every recipe pre-1850, and usually recommended in the small, privately published bread-making books on sale today in specialist food shops. Beating a lot of air into a moist yeast-and-flour mixture certainly creates ideal conditions in which yeast can flourish. As it is not inhibited by the presence of salt, the rising is fairly rapid, which to some cooks may seem advantageous. But this fast rising and subsequent fast risings of the dough mean the flour is not able to ripen and develop its full flavour, and thus the object of many well-intentioned authors — namely, to tell you how to make bread that tastes 'the way it used to be' — is defeated.

The truth is that our ancestors *had* to make bread this way because they had only slow-working yeasts. Their initial sponge-proving could take from two to ten hours. Their later risings also took longer, giving the flavour and gluten a chance to develop most satisfactorily. This is impossible with the 30-40-minute sponge-proving that modern yeast provides, and in any case, only a certain proportion of the flour is being given this time to develop.

The all-in method The introduction of German or compressed yeast of known performance made possible today's simpler and more reliable domestic bread-making practices. It might seem that this way generally requires a bit more kneading

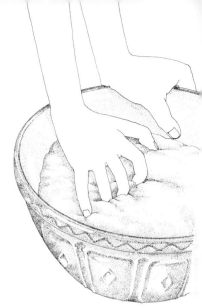

▲ Start mixing by holding the bowl with your left hand and working the ingredients with the right.

muscle, but this is not so. In any case, kneading need not be a chore if you adopt a balanced posture and do it rhythmically.

Moreover, unless you are using all-white flour, long kneading is by no means necessary or advisable. So if you really cannot get used to kneading, always use recipes that are suited to wholemeal flour — or buy a dough hook for your electric mixer.

The all-in method is more flexible than the sponge method, and allows you to fit bread-making easily into your day's programme. By varying the amount of yeast and choosing carefully the temperature in which the dough rises (see p. 86), you can treat bread-making as just another part of routine.

Basic method for kneading

2. First, fold the dough in half by pulling the far side over towards you.

For both greater comfort and more successful kneading, find a surface that is somewhere between hip and mid-thigh height. A wooden board or a laminated work-top are both good, but marble, which is always cold, is not at all suitable.

1. Flour the surface lightly, then tip out the dough, incorporating all the bits and loose flour from the bowl. The dough will look rather weak and uneven; kneading will correct this. Flour your hands lightly and you are ready to start.

5. You will feel the dough slowly respond as it becomes more elastic and able to hold its shape. Add more flour from time to time if it becomes sticky, and continuously incorporate the scraps from the board.

6. When the dough has acquired a satiny texture, a shiny smoothness on the dough, your kneading is complete. Now fold the dough over to you in preparation for setting it to rise for the first time.

3. Smoothly continue this action so the heel of the palm first moves down to the board then pushes on through the dough. Relax your fingers as you get to the other side, at which time the join will be along the top of the dough. Try to follow this action forward with your whole body, or at least your trunk, as this takes all the effort out of kneading.

4. As you rock back again, turn the dough through a quarter circle; this may be done in either direction, with one or two hands, whichever is easiest for you. Now follow the procedure from the start again. Be very subjective about your rhythm and comfort, for the more relaxed you are, the better for you and the dough.

7. Fold it once more to make it about the shape of your warmed, lightly oiled bowl.

9. Cover the bowl with a warmed plate, then cover that with polythene or a thick clean towel. Set the bowl in a suitable place, ensuring that, whatever the temperature you have chosen, the warmth surrounds the bowl evenly and does not come from just one angle.

8. Put the dough into the bowl with the smooth side down, then turn it around, covering the whole surface with a film of oil to prevent a crust forming.

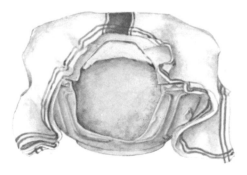

Punching down

It is usual to allow dough to rise until it is about twice its original size. It is this criterion that must be met, rather than any strict adherence to time.

When this stage has been reached it is important to release and redistribute the gas formed by the growth of the yeast. The technique is called punching down: you punch your clenched fist into the middle of the dough and continue until you have a mass just a little bigger than that with which you started. You may like to knead again, too, which is beneficial to the eventual texture.

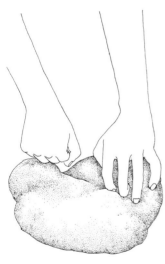

Slapping down

Slapping down is mentioned in many recipes, but there seem to be no universally agreed rules for applying the technique. Simply pick the dough up by one end and slap it down hard on a suitable surface a couple of

times. Then do the same to the other end. It stimulates the yeast into a vigorous new growth in the same way as punching down. If you are determined to bake only with fully-ripened dough you will now let it rise or prove yet again. Otherwise you can start shaping your loaf.

Filling tins

Some cookbooks contain extraordinarily complicated instructions for filling loaf tins. Generally, the complications are in inverse proportion to the aesthetic appeal of the results.

The rules are actually very simple:

(1) Do not fill the tin more than two-thirds full; half-full is better.

(2) Oil or grease and flour the tin, which should be warm.

(3) Unless you are making the two-loaf version of the split-tin loaf (see p. 35), the join of the dough should be on the underside.

To shape each loaf, cut the dough into portions, according to the number and size of the tins. Knead one portion five or six times then roll it into an evenly proportioned log, with the join underneath. If the dough has not adhered to itself at the join, pinch the join firmly together, using a little water. Square off the ends of the loaf with a firm pat or two; use a knife only if necessary. Put the log of dough into the pan and press it lightly but firmly into shape. Using the back of the hand is the most effective method. Now set the dough to rise in a warm place, covered with polythene or a damp towel.

The loaf will be ready for baking when the centre has risen to be level with the top of the tin, or, if the tin was filled two-thirds full, above it.

Shaping, decora- ting and baking

Here are ways to make each loaf exclusively yours: slashing, twisting, plaiting, snipping, sprinkling, flouring and glazing. By making different shapes and using different finishes and decorations you can serve a basket full of imaginative rolls, criss-cross a cob for crusty picnic sandwiches and intrigue your guests with shamrocks, daisies, snails and rosettes.

Cuts and slashes

Professional-looking loaves, shining with glaze, beautifully patterned, dusted with flour or scattered with seeds and grains are well within the scope of even a first-time bread-maker.

For cuts and slashes, all that is required is a really sharp cutting edge, preferably a razor blade, and a confident approach. Cuts are put into dough when it is towards the end of its second rising. Afterwards, the dough is allowed to rest and 're-cover' for about 10 minutes, during which time the cuts will open out well. If this does not happen, the dough was not ready or was not strong enough.

The cuts in French, Vienna and bloomer loaves vary from bakery to bakery but should basically follow the length rather than the width of the loaf. However, on a French loaf, cuts which are too long and deep will simply spread the loaf.

On the bloomer, the cuts should be rather closer together, and if they have a slight 's'-shape, so much the better.

The flour-dusted farmhouse and the split-tin loaf should be slashed deeply at the *start* of the second

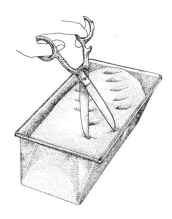

rising, which gives the characteristic very open cut. An alternative way to make the long, split-tin loaf is to fill the tin with two long rolls of dough rather than one. This will automatically produce the required shape.

The so-called Danish loaves are oval-shaped loaves split along the centre with a single cut.

Sharp-ended scissors can be used to make a variety of decorations, but they are perhaps more suitable for using on rolls.

Other bread shapes suited to cutting and decorating are shown overleaf. Flouring, glazing and sprinkling with seeds, etc., are always done after the bread has risen and is just about to go into the oven.

Roll shapes

There are many doughs which have been specially devised for bread rolls, but most bread recipes are also suitable for rolls.

To make roll shapes, you always start with either a rolled strand of dough or a ball. The better you are at these, the better will be your rolls.

As most of the roll shapes are also suitable for loaves, either as individual shapes, like the cottage and coburg, or baked together, like the shamrock and crown, these pages might also encourage you to experiment with new bread shapes and combinations of shapes and designs.

The twist Carefully roll out a length of dough, pull one end around and cross it over the other. Twist the loop on itself and neatly tuck the ends underneath.

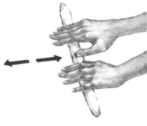

Spirals and swirls Using an even length of dough, make either an exaggerated 's'-shape, twisting the ends in on themselves, or make a spiral by curling the dough, starting on the outside and slightly overlapping each swirl as you work inwards. Curve over the last end and pitch it.

The knotted twist (sometimes called 'flower') Make a longer, thinner version of the twist. Form it into a circle, still twisting; lap one end over and into the centre of the circle.

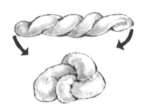

The knot This can be very effective if you make both very small and rather bigger rolls; bake the smaller ones lower in the oven.

The Staffordshire knot

This fascinating shape is very simple: make an ordinary knot at both ends of a strand of dough, then work them close together. Paint just the protruding ends with a milk wash to further disguise the construction.

The rosette This will end up looking similar to the knotted twist but is achieved in a different way. Use a long, and rather thin, strand of dough. Make a circle at one end, about the size you want the roll to be. Twist the longer piece of dough round

the circle, sticking the last bit through the middle. Lightly slashing the top with a sharp knife will improve the rose effect.

The cob This simple shape is traditional for brown rolls topped with cracked wheat and for glazed white rolls of a milk dough. Take care to tuck the edges well under when making this shape, otherwise it will not hold. You could cheat by baking in a patty tin.

The cottage First make two balls of dough, one slightly smaller than the other. Flatten the big ball with the palm and wet slightly on top. Put the second ball on top. Push a finger or spoon handle down into the bottom ball to secure.

The coburg This shape is used mainly for loaves. Do not make the cuts until the dough has risen almost enough to be put in the oven. Make three cuts (one long, two short) and bake as soon as the deep cuts have opened and 'flowered'. Flour the cuts before baking.

The crown This is made in a cake tin, usually with five rolls around the edge and one in the middle. However, this does not produce a very regal effect. To make something more deserving of the name, use cottage rolls instead and glaze them beautifully.

The shamrock This shape is quickly made by shaping a batch of smaller-than-usual round rolls and arranging them in threes. The shamrock works well in patty tins too.

The lattice Follow the instructions for the coburg, but make more cuts to give a crustier finish and then flour them.

The daisy Start with a cottage shape and cut only into the top part. It is best for the top to be about the same diameter but rather less thick than the bottom.

Plaiting

Three strands This is the simplest fancy shape of all. Use it for leaves, rolls or as a decoration to place on top of another loaf.

Start by rolling out three equal strands of dough. Press the ends together with the middle strand on top.

Take the left and right strands alternately and cross them over the middle strand.

When you get to the end, tuck the ends underneath. Plaits always look better if they are glazed.

Five strands This makes a very attractive loaf which looks almost as though you had plaited with plaits.

Arrange five strands of even length, again with the middle one on the top.

Fold the left outside strand over the next two strands, so that it lies in the middle.

Now fold the right outside strand over three strands so that it becomes the second strand from the left.

Continue in this way, folding the left strand over two, the right strand over three.

When you have finished, tuck the ends neatly and, after it has proved, glaze before baking.

Plaits as decorations

As well as plaiting whole loaves, you can decorate with plaits. A small plait along the top of a loaf gives a very attractively shaped slice (see photograph, p. 41).

As an alternative to making a plait of thick strands, use thinner ones and then twist the plait into a circle or garland shape (see p. 75).

Those with patience can plait herbs and spices in with the strands as they work, so that every slice will be different.

Glazing

There are two times at which bread can be glazed—before and after baking. In general, ordinary and savoury breads and plain sweet breads have an egg glaze applied before baking, while fruited tea breads and buns have a sugar glaze brushed on after baking.

Very large loaves can burn if glazed before baking; in such cases it is better to glaze about 20 minutes before the estimated end of the baking time.

Depending on what you have in stock, you can use either cream, milk, egg yolk, whole egg, or egg and milk beaten together for glazing. For a very shiny crisp crust, use egg beaten with salt.

Once you have painted on the glaze you can sprinkle sesame seeds, poppy seeds, caraway, fennel seeds, crushed rock salt or cracked or whole grains (preferably soaked) on top. In the case of fruit breads, currants and other fruit or crushed cube sugar can be used, though all are prone to burn unless

used on small rolls or buns.

Sweet breads, brioches, croissants and so on can be egg-and-milk-glazed before baking but a much higher glaze is obtained by boiling together a few spoonsful of milk and sugar until starting to thicken. Paint this on to the hot bread.

Thin water icing painted or dribbled on to hot pastry or sweet bread gives a good but less startling shine. The matt crust effect is also attractive and not often seen; it is simply achieved by rubbing a little butter on to the loaf while still hot.

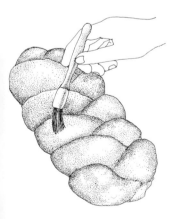

Baking

Most breads bake best in a hot oven—somewhere around 200°C, 400°F/Gas 6. Bake loaves on the centre shelf, rolls nearer the top.

Knowing how your oven behaves and whether there are any fluctuations of power during the day is just as important as following the baking instructions carefully. For this reason you may find that turning down the oven after the first 15 minutes of baking, as some recipes suggest, does not work for you. However, in view of the fact that the old-fashioned bread ovens usually cooked in a gradually diminishing heat, the principle will often hold good, and may help you to avoid a tough-crusted loaf.

Resist the temptation to peer at the bread during those first 15 minutes: opening the oven door may well cause the bread to subside. After 15 minutes, you may want to change its position in the oven if your oven heats unevenly, but do it quickly.

Testing

Most bread baked in tins will come away from the tins when it is almost cooked. A clean teatowel or oven gloves to protect your hands from burns will enable you to tip out the loaf easily. Then, test by tapping it with your knuckles: if you hear a firm hollow sound, the bread is cooked.

It is best to tip moist breads out of their tins two-thirds of the way through cooking and finish them on the baking tray. In this way, the direct heat will reach the centre without over-cooking the crust. However, deft hands are needed to get the loaves out.

Crusty loaves

Sadly, a really crisp crust is almost impossible to obtain in a domestic oven. Crusty loaves require constant steam at exactly the right temperature and finishing in dry heat. The old wood-fired ovens were sprayed with water before the bread was put in and so automatically produced exactly the right type of crust.

Many writers have advised placing a pan of boiling water in the bottom of the oven to produce a good crust. However, in some books this is recommended as a way of achieving a soft crust! Reasonable results can be achieved by removing the pan of water 10-15 minutes before the end of cooking.

Spraying liberally with water just before baking works rather better; salty water is better still.

Professional bakers use a ploy that you could copy in your own home as an alternative. They bake the bread under either a bowl or a tall, metal cylinder, which means that the bread cooks in its own steam, as it did in the very earliest sealed clay ovens. To copy this at home, you will need firm dough, a baking sheet and an oven-proof bowl, such as a Pyrex dish or casserole, big enough to cover the loaf and allow it to rise without touching the sides—it is not a mould or container but an oven within an oven.

Let the bread prove or rise the second time under such a cover, remove it to make any cuts or to glaze it, then replace it and put the whole assemblage into an oven a little hotter than usual, say 230°C, 450°F/Gas 8. It must bake for half an hour before you check the loaf, which must be done with extreme caution. Remove the baking tray with the bread and bowl upon it. Lever off the bowl, using a spatula. The bread should have increased in size rather more than usual but will not yet be browning. Put it back in the oven for another 15-30 minutes depending on the size of the loaf.

Cooling and storing
The cooling of the loaves should be as even as possible, but because the bread is constantly losing moisture it must not be left out to cool any longer than necessary. Cooling on a rack is best; alternatively, stand the loaf to cool across the tin in which it was baked; this sets up a sort of barrier of warm air from the tin.

There are two great fallacies concerning bread storage: one concerns refrigeration and the other concerns air. Although refrigeration will certainly slow down the appearance and growth of mould, it will also hasten the departure of moisture, particularly when the bread is in a plastic bag. It also affects granulation of the starch giving a hard crumb.

The reason why refrigerated bread feels moist is simply that it *is* refrigerated, and therefore attracts condensation from the warmer atmosphere into which it is introduced. By heating the refrigerated bread in a hot oven for 10 minutes you can return the starch to a softer state and so render the bread far tastier.

Surprisingly enough, bread keeps better if there is circulation of air. The reason is simple. In a space without an air-flow there will be a build-up of the moisture given off by the bread. A moist atmosphere is a basic requirement for the growth of mould: the more tightly the bread is sealed, the better the chances of it going mouldy.

Any container that can easily be washed and cleaned and that is not porous is suitable for bread storage. If you have a bread bin that does not allow circulation of air, prop the lid open with a few pieces of cork.

Simply wrapping bread in a clean teatowel and storing it on a cool, airy shelf is just as effective.

Deep freezing and its advantages are discussed on pp. 89-90.

▶ Fancy breads don't always need fancy doughs. This traditional wheatsheaf was made with 100% wholemeal flour. Ingenuity in combining shapes, glazes, textures and grains will all give individuality. The grains and flours shown here are (right to left) wheat, rye, oat flakes, millet, cracked wheat and rye flour.

Bread without yeast

By following in the footsteps of the earliest bakers, you can make breads that do not need yeast. Unleavened flat breads serve as plates and forks in India and Mexico. Soda breads can come to your rescue in an emergency. Sour-dough breads bring old-world flavours to your table. With these techniques, you need never be without bread, even on mountain-tops or deserted beaches.

Unleavened bread

Chapati

The lighter and larger the chapati, the better the cook is judged to be.

450 g (1 lb) wholemeal flour
water
butter or ghee (clarified
     butter)

Make fairly stiff dough with the flour and water and knead very well—for at least 8 minutes. Cover with a damp cloth and leave for about 2 hours. Knead again.

Break off pieces of dough about the size of an egg, incorporate a smear of butter or ghee, flatten, then roll out very thinly between sheets of greaseproof paper or baking foil.

Chapatis should be cooked on an extremely hot cast-iron griddle, failing which cook them under a grill. Cook one side for just a few seconds, turn, then press the outer edges with a clean cloth—or with a spatula if cooking under a grill—to encourage the chapatis to puff up.

Serve immediately or keep moist by smearing a little butter or ghee on one side after cooking and wrapping in a clean cloth. If left unwrapped, the chapatis will be drier and more absorbent, therefore best served with moist food.

Variations Plain flour can be substituted for wholemeal. Blend 25 g (1 oz) butter into the flour and start mixing the dough with 40-60 ml (3-4 tablespoons) milk, then finish using water. Make the chapatis slightly thicker than usual.

Chapatis can be cooked three at a time, with a layer of flour and brushing of melted butter between each to separate them. If doing this, cook as above but for longer at a lower temperature, and cut into pieces for serving.

Paratha

Make thin pancakes from the wholemeal chapati dough, brush with melted butter or ghee and fold in half. Brush again, fold once more and roll into a fan shape. Cook on a hot griddle or under a grill. A little extra fat can be used to make the parathas brown.

Variations Roll out two small, thicker pancakes. Brush with butter, put about 25 g (1 oz) spicy vegetable purée in the middle of one. Place the other on top, seal the edges, roll out to make as large and as thin a paratha as possible without the stuffing bursting through.

Pooris

These are chapatis which have been deep-fried in vegetable fat. They puff up and need careful draining.

Tortilla

Tortillas are the simple basis for a wide range of fascinating foods.

225 g (8 oz) masa harina* or
     corn meal
water to mix
salt (only if desired)

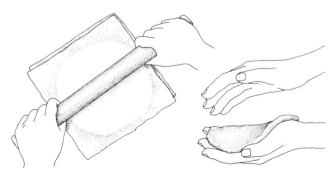

Masa harina, which is made from corn cooked in lime-water, is not commonly available outside Mexico, though certain American companies do export it to the UK. Ordinary corn meal is an acceptable substitute.

Slowly make a firm dough with the flour and water, adding the water gradually (the amount needed depends to some extent on atmospheric conditions).

Tear off pieces of dough about the size of a golf ball. Experts slap them into shape between the hands; novices are advised to roll them out between sheets of grease-proof paper or baking foil until as thin as possible and about 10 cm (4 in) across.

Cook on a dry griddle or in a frying-pan for just 1 minute per side, turning when the edges lift and the tortillas are patchily brown underneath.

Tacos

These are fried tortillas, which keep better than the basic tortillas and can be filled in many different ways.

Using tacos and tortillas

The Mexicans usually fill tacos with shredded lettuce, tomato and grated cheese, plus a little spicy meat: minced meat with extra garlic and chilli powder stirred in is typical; chicken, paprika sausages, chilli with or without meat, bacon and leftover curry also work.

Tortillas can also be filled, rolled and baked, like cannelloni, or layered like lasagne.

Swedish rye crisps

1 kg (2 lb) floury potatoes
5 g (1 level teaspoon) salt
about 340 g (12 oz) rye flour

Boil the potatoes in their jackets, cool slightly then peel. Chop roughly and sieve.

Add the salt, then knead in the rye flour to form a stiff, rather sticky dough. Take portions of the dough and roll out paper-thin on a well-floured board. Cut into shapes, then prick all over.

Heat a thick frying-pan or griddle, grease very lightly and cook the crisps both sides. They may be shaped into rolls after being removed from the pan.

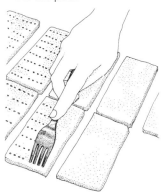

Crusaders' bread

This bread is still made in the Bible lands, and also in France and Belgium.

275 ml (10 fl oz) clear honey, slightly warmed
about 225 g (8 oz) flour

For something akin to the biblical cake of flour and honey, use Israeli orange-blossom honey and 85% flour with a scattering of buckwheat or buckwheat flour, also known as saracen flour.

Gradually work the flour into the warmed honey, in a bowl, to make a stiff paste (the atmosphere and the quality of the honey will determine the amount of flour).

Roll the paste between two sheets of greaseproof paper or baking foil to about 1 cm ($\frac{1}{2}$ in) thick. Cover, then allow to stand at comfortable room temperature for at least two days, during which time it will rise slightly.

Use a cutter to make discs of 10-15 cm (4-6 in) in diameter. Wooden moulds or a greased knife can be used to emboss patterns on the surfaces.

Bake at 150°C, 300°F/Gas 2 for about 25 minutes until just browning.

This bread will keep indefinitely in an airtight container.

Variations 5-10 g (1-2 teaspoons) baking powder can be added to the paste so that the bread can be baked immediately. If this is done, a little brown sugar and cinnamon should be added to compensate for the flavour lost by not maturing the mixture.

Dutch rye

This is a heavy, chewy bread of the 'brick pumpernickel' type.

450 g (1 lb) cracked or coarse rye meal

125 g (4 oz) cracked wheat (sometimes sold as kibbled wheat)

5 g (1 level teaspoon) salt

15 g (1 level tablespoon) molasses

15 ml (1 tablespoon) oil

25 g (1 oz) bran or wholemeal flour

boiling water

Mix all the ingredients together, then add boiling water to make a thick, porridgy batter. Leave overnight, covered. Add bran or wholemeal flour if extra body is required to shape the dough into a firm loaf. Put into a loaf tin and seal with baking foil. Cook for at least 2 hours in a low oven (100°C, 200°F/Gas $\frac{1}{4}$). Cool in the pan. This bread is best left several days before cutting.

Exercise bread

This healthy mixture needs hearty chewing!

450 g (1 lb) wholemeal flour

225 g (8 oz) buckwheat flour

225 g (8 oz) corn meal

225 g (8 oz) cooked brown rice

5 g (1 level teaspoon) salt

150 ml (5 fl oz) oil

sesame seeds

Mix the flours, meal, rice and salt. Knead in the oil until it is evenly distributed. Leave to rest for 1-2 hours, or alternatively overnight, in which case it will rise a little.

Now add a little water until the dough is slightly sticky. Shape and place in an oiled pan. Sprinkle with sesame seeds. Leave covered in a warm place for an hour, then bake at 190°C, 375°F/Gas 5 for 1-1$\frac{1}{2}$ hours.

Dampers

The Boy Scouts' favourite camp-fire food is capable of tasting rather better than you might think!

The basic technique is to make a very firm dough of flour and water, roll it into strips, wrap these round twigs (preferably green), and cook them over an open fire. This can be done either by poking one end of the stick into the ground a sensible distance from the fire (so that the bread cooks rather than burns) or by placing the stick across two forked twigs stuck into the ground on either side of the fire. Rotate the stick from time to time.

For a superior damper, add some baking powder to make prairie bread (p. 48), baked over the fire or in the ashes. Or cook the mixture, which should be even firmer than usual, on the stick.

For a camping holiday of some length, it is worth preparing some sour-dough starter before departure (p. 44). Or put some un-cooked damper dough to one side, protected from the ravages of insects and heavy boots, to use as a sour-dough leavener after 2-3 days.

Sour-dough breads

Sour-dough bread is leavened with a proportion of a previously-made dough. This dough, the sour-dough starter, will have been left in a warm place to turn sour and create gas. Once such a starter has been made, it will keep indefinitely, but it is better to bake regularly, replenishing the starter each time.

The last sour-dough recipe in the sequence below is a modern 'cheat', for it uses vinegar to help achieve the same style of flavour as real sour-dough.

SOUR-DOUGH STARTERS

Traditionally, starters were very simple, just flour and milk with water.

To make a simple starter, mix together equal quantities of flour and milk (an average teacup- or breakfast-cupful is about right). Use wheat flour (whole or white), rye flour, or a mixture. Aim for a thick batter; thin with some water if required then stir in 10 g (2 teaspoons) sugar.

Leave uncovered for 2-3 days in a warm place.

The more sophisticated starters which follow give better results.

Potato starter

up to 450 g (1 lb) large
   potatoes, scrubbed but
   not peeled
450 g (1 lb) flour
50 g (2 oz) sugar
10 g (2 level teaspoons)
   salt

Boil the potatoes, just covered with water. Peel, then mash in the cooking water. Mix in the flour (any mixture of flours will do; rye is excellent), sugar and salt.

Put into an earthenware bowl and cover. After about 4 days in a warm place the mixture will become bubbly and have a strong smell. It is then ready for use.

Yeasted starter

25 g (1 oz) fresh yeast or $\frac{1}{2}$
   as much dried yeast
575 ml (20 fl oz) warm
   water
20 g (2 level teaspoons)
   honey*
340 g (12 oz) flour
*sugar can be used instead

Dissolve the yeast in some of the water with the honey. Mix in the flour and make a thick paste of it. Leave to ferment for at least 4 days, stirring back any liquid that rises.

Having grown a starter, the sour-dough bread-making can be planned. The two-stage sponge method can be followed with advantage; proving the sponge overnight improves the flavour even more. A great deal, however, will depend on the strength of the starter.

Sour-dough wholemeal
Evening session:
   225 g (8 oz) starter
   ·5 kg (1 lb 2 oz)
      wholemeal flour
   1 litre (1$\frac{3}{4}$ pints) warm
      water

Add the starter to the flour, then add the water until a

thick porridgy batter is formed. Beat well with a

wooden spoon. Cover and leave overnight in a moderately warm place.

Morning session:
   100 ml (4 fl oz) cooking
      oil
   25 g (1 oz) salt
   ·7 kg (1$\frac{1}{2}$ lb) flour
      (either strong white or
      rye)

First, remove about 225 g (8 oz) of the risen sponge and incorporate it into the original starter. Cover and place in the refrigerator.

Fold the oil, then the finely ground salt, into the sponge. Work in the flour to give a dough that is rather slacker than a yeasted dough. Knead for 5 minutes, adding more flour if it is too sticky.

Form into two loaves and prove for about 2 hours in well-oiled tins. If using rye flour, shape into flattish rounds instead. Bake for 20 minutes at 220°C, 425°F/Gas 7, then turn down the heat to 190°C, 375°F/Gas 5 and bake for at least 30 minutes longer.

Variations French bread is often made this way, using a sour-dough starter of unbleached white flour and substituting this flour in the sponge and mix too. P. 53 shows how to roll a French loaf correctly.

Sour-dough rye bread

Sour-dough is unquestionably the best way of making a rye loaf, according to the Middle-Europeans. This is one of the simplest recipes for sour-dough rye bread.

225 g (8 oz) starter
2 litres (4 pints) potato
water (see p. 45)
approx. 1·5 kg (3·31 lb) rye
flour
25 g (1 oz) salt
100 g (4 fl oz) molasses or
honey
25 g (1 oz) caraway seeds
(optional)

Add the starter to the liquids and half the flour. Mix, cover and stand for 3 hours in a warm place. Leave to sour longer if desired.

Stir well, then remove 225 g (8 oz) of the mixture to replenish the starter. Add the rest of the ingredients to the remaining sponge to make a rather stiff dough.

Knead on a floured board until no longer sticky. Shape into loaves and leave to prove, covered with a damp cloth, on a greased baking sheet. This may take 4 hours, but your patience will be rewarded.

Bake at 180°C, 350°F/Gas 4 for 1 hour and then test: they may need longer.

Variations Leave out the caraway. Substitute scalded milk for the potato water (scalded milk can be used if you think the dough is too stiff in any case).

If the bread is a bit heavy for your taste, substitute strong white or 85% flour for 50% or more of the rye flour. This may alter your starter's flavour and composition.

Cheat's sour-dough

This is the basis for several West Coast (USA) bread recipes.

15 g ($\frac{1}{2}$ oz) fresh yeast or $\frac{1}{2}$
as much dried yeast
50 ml (2 fl oz) warm water
5 g (1 level teaspoon) salt
1 large egg
25 ml (1 fl oz) cider vinegar
350 g (12 oz) strong white
flour

Add the yeast to the warm water and after 10 minutes add in the salt and liquid ingredients and half the flour. Pile the rest of the flour on a board, then work in the first mixture to make a soft dough. Knead lightly (working in and kneading should take about 5 minutes).

Shape into a round and place in an oiled 22-cm (9-in) cake tin. Allow to double in size, then bake for 1 hour at 180°C, 350°F/Gas 4.

Variations Add more egg or cider vinegar, or about 5 g (1 teaspoon) raw sugar or molasses.

Using a sour-dough starter

Once you make a starter it can last indefinitely if you replenish it each time you make bread.

225 g (8 oz)
starter

liquids
and
flour

starter bowl

225 g (8 oz)
dough mixture
back into starter
bowl

mixture kneaded, shaped
into loaf or loaves
and left to prove

dough bowl

46

Soda breads

Soda breads are both easy and delicious. Success will be assured if you (1) use sour milk or buttermilk and (2) eat the finished bread as soon as humanly possible. (If you have only sweet milk, substitute baking powder for soda and double the quantity.) Soda breads re-heat fairly well but will not taste quite the same, even as little as 24 hours after being baked.

Wholemeal soda bread
This is a specially good way to enjoy wholemeal flavour.

500 g (just over 1 lb) wholemeal flour
10 g (2 level teaspoons) salt
5-8 g (1½ teaspoons) bicarbonate of soda
250 ml (10 fl oz) soured buttermilk or milk
warm water

Sift the flour, salt and bicarbonate of soda twice to ensure a thorough mix. Work in the sour buttermilk or milk (it must be sharp and clean, without any offensive smell), working in as quickly as possible. Lukewarm water can be added in if the dough is too stiff; hot water will over-activate the soda and lead to disaster.

Soda breads are usually shaped into a flattish round and marked with a deep cross.

Put the shaped dough on a floured baking sheet and straight into a hot oven (230°C, 450°F/Gas 8) for about half an hour. Soda breads may be cooked under an inverted cake tin, which should be large enough for the dough not to be in contact with it and removed about two-thirds of the way through cooking, so that the crust can brown.

Variations This kind of bread can be enriched with lard, especially if white flour is substituted for wholemeal: 25 g (1 oz) lard is enough for 500 g (just over 1 lb) white flour, which may be strong or soft. The amount of soda should be doubled (or 5 g/1 level teaspoon cream of tartar added). The bread should be cooled on a wire rack.

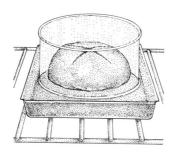

Boston brown bread
Soda breads often used to be steamed in tightly closed containers. This is the most famous of the steamed soda breads, from the east coast of the USA.

100 g (4 oz) each of wholemeal flour, corn meal and rye flour
10 g (2 level teaspoons) baking soda
5 g (1 level teaspoon) salt
175 ml (6 fl oz) molasses
425 ml (15 fl oz) sour milk

Mix the dry ingredients very well. Stir the molasses into the milk. Combine the two mixtures, then pour the combination into well-greased tin moulds. This mix makes two loaves steamed in tins of 700-900-g (1¾-2-lb) capacity. Seal the moulds well (cooking foil and string will do) and stand them in a large saucepan on a trivet or upturned saucer in cold water that reaches about two-thirds of the way up the containers' sides. Once the water has boiled, cook the bread gently for 2-3 hours; dough in tall, thin containers cooks faster than dough in something squat. Add more boiling water as necessary.

Remove each container from the water, take off the seal and put the tins into a medium-hot oven to dry. After about 10 minutes, remove the bread from the tins, then put back into the oven to crisp (about 30 minutes).

Old American cookbooks recommend that this bread is eaten with plates of hearty Boston baked beans, as a pudding with sweetened sour cream and nutmeg or as a hot tea-bread. If using it as a tea-bread, add a handful of raisins when mixing and, if desired, substitute fine oatmeal for the rye flour.

If you wish to try steaming wholemeal soda bread, you can put your container straight into boiling water, but starting in cold water is more traditional. The well-greased top of a double-boiler could also be used. Whatever container you use, do not fill it more than two-thirds full.

Corn bread

This can be steamed or baked: most people will find baking more convenient. Always include buttermilk or sour milk and some quantity of egg, and put the batter into a very hot, greased shallow pan in order to obtain a crisp undercrust.

Spoon bread is another name for corn bread. It is all eaten from the pan, straight from the oven, the diners helping themselves with a spoon. Spoon bread is also called pone.

15 g (1 level tablespoon) white flour
2-3 g (½ teaspoon) baking soda
5 g (1 level teaspoon) baking powder
2-3 g (½ teaspoon) salt
15 g (1 level tablespoon) sugar
125 g (4 oz) corn meal
1 egg
225 ml (8 fl oz) sour milk
15 ml (1 level tablespoon) melted butter

Mix flour, soda, baking powder, salt and sugar. Sift into corn meal and mix lightly. Beat egg and add to milk; mix into dry ingredients, then add melted butter. Turn into a heated, greased 24-cm (9-in) pie dish. Place immediately in an oven at 220°C, 425°F/Gas 7 for about 30 minutes.

Serve straight from the oven. If you use sweet milk, use 15 ml (3 teaspoons) baking powder and omit the soda.

Country oat bread

This is a relatively sweet bread that needs lashings of butter or, even better, home-made jam and whipped cream.

125 g (4 oz) rolled oats
425 ml (15 fl oz) scalded milk
1 egg
350 g (12 oz) wholemeal flour
5 g (1 level teaspoon) salt
150 g (5 oz) sugar
25 g (1 oz) baking powder

Soak the oats in the hot milk until cool. Beat up the egg. Sift the flour, salt, sugar and baking powder into a bowl, add the oats and egg and mix well. Put into a greased tin and leave to stand for 20 minutes. Bake at 180°C, 350°F/Gas 4 for about 1½ hours. Serve warm rather than hot.

Prairie bread

This is an American pioneer recipe for present-day campers and those who cannot make sour-dough work.

225 g (8 oz) any white flour
25 g (4-5 teaspoons) baking powder
10 g (2 teaspoons) sugar
5 g (1 level teaspoon) salt
50 g (2 oz) butter or lard
275 ml (10 fl oz) water
(The measurements are not critical.)

Sift or mix well the flour, baking powder, sugar and salt. Then chop the butter or lard and gently rub it into the flour until the mixture looks like fine breadcrumbs. Add the water and mix well. Grease a 25-cm (10-in) frying-pan or other suitably heavy pan, ideally with bacon fat.

Pour in the mixture and cook it *very* slowly over a low heat. When the bread has stopped rising, which it will do only slowly, check to see if it is well browned on the bottom. If it is, turn the bread over in the pan, even though the top will seem rather wet. Cook this side (about 15 minutes each side is normal). Serve hot with plenty of butter.

Ember and ash bread

If you are camping 'rough' and have only an open fire to cook on, you can still enjoy home-baked bread. Soda breads can be cooked in a sealed tin (as long as the top permits you to get the cooked bread out) or in a similar heatproof container standing in the raked-out ashes of a fire.

Alternatively, rake out the ashes, make a nest about the size of the dough, leaving a good base of hot embers, and put the dough into the nest. Let it set and form a crust, then carefully cover it with ashes and leave it for 30 minutes or so. This can also be done at home, in the hearth.

▶ Clockwise from the top: prairie bread, wholemeal soda bread, sour-dough rye, tortillas, tacos, Boston brown bread.

Yeasted breads

Once you have perfected your basic doughs, you can exercise your imagination by adding in sweet or savoury extras, forming the dough into unusual shapes and using different glazes and decorations. The flavour of buckwheat will complement game, barbecues are a good excuse for a savoury plait and all children love fruit breads: make the most of opportunities to ring the changes on the basic loaf.

The wholemeal loaf

Wholemeal bread can be stodgy and tough-crusted, which are not qualities of good bread no matter what the health-food fanatics may maintain! Goodness does not need to go hand in hand with culinary masochism.

The problem of stodgy wholemeal bread is likely to be the amount of liquid used: almost every packet of wholemeal flour on the market will require different proportions. The best way to ensure wholemeal bread of good texture and palatable crust is to aim for consistently-textured dough each time, rather than using consistent quantities. If you are still unsuccessful, revert to wholemeal soda bread.

▲ Sprinkle cracked wheat into greased tins before you put in the dough.

No-knead loaf

900 g (2 lb) 100%
  wholemeal flour
15 g ($\frac{1}{2}$ oz) salt
25 g (1 oz) fresh yeast or $\frac{1}{2}$
  as much dried yeast
625-700 ml (22-24 fl oz)
  lukewarm water
15 g ($\frac{1}{2}$ oz) dark muscavado
  or Barbados sugar

Warm the flour and salt in a low oven. Activate the yeast in some of the warm water, adding a pinch of white sugar if using dried yeast. Add the brown sugar when it starts to work.

Pour the yeast into a well in the centre of the flour, then add most of the rest of the water. Mix well for 1-2 minutes with a wooden spoon. The mixture should be fairly soft and wet, so add more water if necessary. Put the dough straight into oiled tins—1 large or 2 small. Cover the tins and let the dough rise by about one-third to one-half. It is worth marking the tin so that you know when this has happened, for too much or too little rising can affect this bread badly.

Bake the bread at 205°C, 400°F/Gas 6 for 30-35 minutes (small) or 45 minutes (large). To test whether it is cooked, tap the top: if it is, it will sound hollow. Turn out the loaves to cool on a

cooling tray or across the tins. Providing it is stored properly, this bread will continue to improve in flavour for several days.

Double the quantities of this recipe when you are confident of a good result, but use only 40 g ($1\frac{1}{2}$ oz) yeast.

Variations A little milk, butter, lard, margarine or oil in the mixture softens the crumb and delays staling. 50 g (2 oz) butter or oil is more than ample in a double-quantities recipe, and similarly you need only a spoonful or two of milk.

Jordan loaf

Using the proportions of the previous recipe with half the amount of salt and the addition of 15 g (1 dessert-spoon) malt extract will produce the loaf recommended by the Jordans, one of England's few remaining families to run a mill on traditional lines. They recommend that the dough is kneaded for 3 minutes or so until the texture is felt to change. The dough is divided into two small tins, left to rise well above the sides of the tins, then baked at 205°C, 400°F/Gas 6 for 10 minutes and at 180°C, 350°F/Gas 4 for 30-40 minutes.

In wholemeal bread-making the dough *must* be at the same temperature from the beginning to the baking—so do not add very hot water and then let it cool, and do not start with warm water then put the dough in a very hot place. Slow, even growth of the yeast and ripening of the flour is the main goal. Wholemeal breads are almost always better baked in tins as they are rather 'slack' doughs. If you want to shape the loaves, incorporate some strong white flour or use 85% flour: these will require kneading, and the bread will therefore acquire more body.

Middle-of-the-road bread

For a change from either white or wholemeal, try bread made with 85% flour. It is the ideal foil for most foods and can easily be adapted to make different 'fancy' loaves, even fruity ones. To give it different sorts of textures, add 100% wholemeal flour or strong white flour.

Bread made with 85% flour (or 81%, according to the manufacturer) is specially suited to long ripening and is much more rewarding for that single reason. It is an ideal bread to fit into a daily routine, too.

1 kg (about 2 lb 4 oz) 85% or 81% flour
25 g (1 oz) fresh yeast or $\frac{1}{2}$ as much dried yeast
25 g (1 oz) salt
about 575 ml (20 fl oz) lukewarm water

While the flour is warming in a low oven, activate the yeast with a little of the warm water. (sugar is necessary only if you are using dried yeast). Mix the salt into the flour. Pour the creamy yeast into the centre of the flour, add a splash of water and start mixing with your hands. Gradually work in the water until a firm dough is produced.

Turn on to a floured board and knead until the dough changes texture and has a satin-smooth appearance. Put it into a warmed, lightly oiled bowl, cover and leave for 1$\frac{1}{2}$-2 hours to double in size. Punch down, slap a couple of times and then knead lightly until you feel it 'coming back to life'.

The second kneading ensures a good second rising and a lighter loaf.

Shape the dough into two portions suitable for large loaf tins. Cover and allow to double in size. Bake at 220°C, 425°F/Gas 7 for 15 minutes, then turn heat down to 205°C, 400°F/Gas 6 for another 15 minutes.

Remove from the tin and bake for a final 15-20 minutes at 180°C, 350°F/Gas 4. The bread will be ready when tapping it on the underside produces a hollow sound. Cool on a rack.

Variations The bread will be improved by an extra kneading and proving, which makes it taste better and gives a lighter texture. A little butter or milk can be added to the loaf if desired. As long as the dough is not made too slack and wet, it can be used to make any number of shapes, including the bloomer shape.

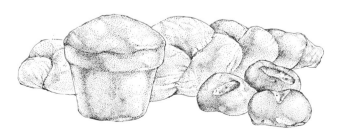

White breads

There will always be occasions when only white bread seems appropriate. Certainly a glazed plait, slashed loaf, floury coburg or cottage loaf would make a wonderful centre-piece for any meal. Even if your table arrangements are not of prime importance, it is as well to ring the changes from time to time. Here is a good basic white bread recipe, followed by one for the new-fangled, short-time bread.

Basic white bread
Makes one 1-kg (2·2-lb) loaf or two 500-g (1-lb) loaves
15 g ($\frac{1}{2}$ oz) fresh yeast or $\frac{1}{2}$ as much dried yeast
425 ml (15 fl oz) warm water or mixture of milk and water
50 g (2 oz) lard or butter
10 g (2 level teaspoons) salt
675 g (24 oz) strong white flour

Activate the yeast in a little of the liquid, adding a pinch of sugar if using dried yeast. Melt the fat in the remaining liquid and add the salt. Add the yeast when creamy, pouring it slowly over the warmed flour. Mix in well to make a firm dough.

Knead very thoroughly until the dough is elastic but no longer sticky—perhaps 10 minutes.

Leave to rise, covered, in a warm place until about double in size. The dough will spring back when pressed lightly with a floured finger.

Punch down and knead again until the dough is firm. Shape and finish as you wish then leave to rise again until doubled in size.

Bake at 230°C,450°F/Gas 8 for 45-50 minutes for the large loaf, 30-40 minutes for the two small loaves.

Short-time white bread
The addition of a small amount of Vitamin C (ascorbic acid) allows you to make white bread of acceptable taste and texture with just one rising. You can have a finished loaf within 2 hours of starting. Only fresh yeast can be used for this bread because dried yeast extends the rising time by an hour or so, defeating the object of the recipe.

25 g (1 oz) fresh yeast
400 ml (14 fl oz) warm water
25 mg ascorbic acid
15 g ($\frac{1}{2}$ oz) butter or lard
675 g (24 oz) strong white flour
15 g ($\frac{1}{2}$ oz) salt
5 g (1 level teaspoon) sugar

Mix the yeast, water and crushed tablet of ascorbic acid. Melt the butter or lard and add to the liquid. Add to the warmed flour, salt and sugar. Mix together, turn out and knead thoroughly until the texture changes. Leave the dough to rest for about 5 minutes.

Shape the dough, either in tins or into plaits, cobs, rolls—whatever you like.

Leave, covered, to rise. This will take 40-50 minutes (less for rolls).

Brush with beaten egg or dust with flour if you want a farmhouse effect. Bake at 230°C,450°F/Gas 8 for 30-35 minutes (15-20 minutes for rolls).

Variations Both the basic and the short-time loaf can easily be enriched by using milk or egg in the mixture. Each egg reduces the amount of liquid required, so be careful.

Both types of bread are ideal for decorating with slits and cuts and with seeds of all kinds, and both lend themselves admirably to being converted to the sweet, savoury, spiced and stuffed breads that appear later in this book. In the days of once-a-week batch-baking at home, a portion of the basic dough was always put to one side for such treats. This can be done even with small amounts of dough.

French stick

Unless you use true French flour, which is difficult to find outside France, you cannot make a true French loaf. French flour is softer than that of most other countries, therefore it absorbs less water. That, together with the fact that additives and bleaching are completely banned in France, is why true French stick bread goes stale so quickly. So all that will normally be possible in the UK is French-*style* bread. Having accepted the limitations, you can use any recipe that suits and concentrate on making it look right! One way to achieve a very thin loaf is to roll the dough out flat and thin then roll that up. Shorter, thicker loaves are also attractive when made like this but should be rolled up like a croissant, corner to corner. This shape is preferable for loaves made from dough that contains milk and are to be sprinkled with poppy seed. The size of your oven will determine the length of your French loaf. Special baking containers for keeping the sticks apart are available from specialist kitchenware shops.

Your ability to make professional-looking slashes will complete the deception. The cuts should be made during the second rising (or, with short-time dough, the only rising), shortly before you reckon the bread is ready for baking.

The secret is to make long cuts that are slanted considerably more *along* the loaf than across it. Let the loaves recover for 10 minutes or so after cutting, by which time the cuts will have opened and matured well. A good spray with cold water over the cuts will help ensure a good crust. Be careful not to over-bake these thin loaves.

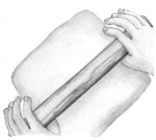

▲ (1a) For a long even loaf, roll the dough into a thin oblong.

▲ (1b) Roll up quite tightly so it will fit your baking tray.

▲ (1c) Prove on a lightly greased tray then slash (see right).

▲ (2a) For a fat, tapering loaf, start rolling from one corner.

▲ (2b) Roll with extra pressure to even up the shape.

▲ (2c) Cut long diagonals with a sharp knife or razor blade prior to baking.

53

Pitta

Pitta, one of the world's most popular breads, originated in the Middle East. Its distinctive taste and texture are produced by the large amount of oil it contains and the high temperature at which it is cooked. Pitta is best served hot.

15 g ($\frac{1}{2}$ oz) fresh yeast or
  $\frac{1}{2}$ as much dried yeast
150 ml (5 fl oz) warm water
450 g (1 lb) strong white
  flour
5 g (1 teaspoon) salt
approx. 150 ml (5 fl oz)
  peanut or sunflower oil

Activate the yeast in some water, adding a pinch of sugar if using dried yeast. When frothy, add to the warmed mixture of flour and salt with the remaining water. Mix well, then add the oil slowly. Expect a rather firm dough. Knead for at least 15 minutes. Leave to double in size, knock down, knead lightly and shape into pieces the size of tennis balls.

Roll out into an oval shape with a floured rolling pin until 0·75 cm ($\frac{1}{4}$ in) thick. Leave covered while heating the oven at maximum temperature for 20 minutes.

Slide the pittas on to a baking sheet, sprinkle with water and bake for 7 minutes at the top of the oven. Do not open the oven door during cooking.

Remove from the oven and cool on racks to prevent sweating. Provided the oven was hot enough the pittas will have puffed up, kept their shapes and be slightly crisp.

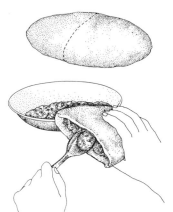

Pitta can be torn into pieces and used as a dip or scoop, or cut in half to produce two steaming pockets of bread. Fill with hot kebabs, grilled spicy sausages, or cold sliced meats plus a finely chopped salad of lettuce, tomato, cucumber, onion and garlic. Taramasalata, houmous and Greek garlic and vegetable dips go well with pitta.

Variations Wholemeal flour can be used instead of strong white; for a sweeter bread, use ordinary household flour and somewhat less liquid.

Greek sesame bread

You can make Greek-style bread with any of the foregoing white-dough recipes, but the flavour will be more authentic if you do not use milk or egg in the mixture.

A good portion of oil, say up to one-third, can be substituted for water. The dough should be exceptionally well kneaded and a little on the soft side. Shape the

bread into a large disc. Just before it is ready to be baked, cut a circle right round the loaf. Spray or sprinkle the loaf with water and scatter sesame seeds over the loaf. Using very salty water to wet the loaf gives the sesame seeds an extra savoury taste.

In Greece, sticks are also made like this.

Using other grains and flours

By experimenting with mixtures of flour and additives of grains, you can create your very own loaf. Often these flavours will be too individual to become your daily bread, but will work well within the context of a meal.

Whole grains

This is a simple, attractive way to give breads a lift, and works specially well in a base of 85% flour. It is best to soak the whole grains overnight to soften them up a little. Then you may incorporate them in the dough without changing other proportions radically.

If you wish to add a lot of whole grains, you should swap about 10% of your flour for rye flour, which helps the texture a lot. Almost any whole grain can be used, including such rarities as millet and linseed, as well as the lightly cracked grains, or rolled oats.

For a less chewy grain, cook it through first and take care not to add too much liquid to the dough.

Other flours

Rye flour is first choice for mixtures. Although making a heavy dough all by itself, because of its very low gluten content, it adds wonderful sweetness and 'lift' to almost any other dough.

Corn meal softens the crumb but adds fragrance.

Rice flour makes bread rather dense. Brown-rice flour, more difficult to find, adds sweetness. Cooked rice is an interesting addition, too.

Buckwheat really is another world of flavour. Associated with the buckwheat pancakes and maple syrup of North America, it is also popular, under the name of saracen wheat, in Belgium and Northern France.

Malted grains, usually wheat grains, are what give so-called 'granary' bread its special flavour. Prepared flour containing such grains is often more easily available than the grains themselves. Some pre-packed bread mixes, containing dry yeast and 'granary grains', make rather good bread of this kind.

Standen loaf

The Standen loaf is from an English country house with Canadian associations.

25 g (1 oz) fresh yeast or
  $\frac{1}{2}$ as much dried yeast
425 ml (15 fl oz) lukewarm
  water
150 ml (5 fl oz) scalded milk
25 g (1 oz) honey
25 g (1 oz) malt extract
25 g (1 oz) salt
900 g (2 lb) 85% flour
225 g (8 oz) buckwheat
  flour

Activate the yeast in some of the warm water, adding a pinch of sugar if using dried yeast. Add the milk to the remaining water, then dissolve the honey, malt extract and salt in it. Make a well in the middle of the previously mixed and warmed flours, then work in the two liquids. Turn out and knead on a floured board to get a dough of medium consistency and satiny appearance. This can either be allowed to rise, punched down and shaped, or shaped immediately. Put the dough into 1 large or 2 small tins and cover with a damp cloth until it has risen well.

Bake at about 200°C, 400°F/Gas 6 for 10 minutes then reduce the temperature to 180°C, 350°F/Gas 4 and bake for another 30-40 minutes. Serve with game or at breakfast with bacon and eggs.

Variations If you find the loaf a little sweet you could replace the honey with a small spoonful of brown sugar and a touch more malt extract. Molasses would work well in this bread, too.

To match up the Canadian affinities, try using maple syrup, either real or artificial.

Rice bread

By changing the type of rice and flour used, this recipe can be widely varied. Basmatti rice or brown rice with wholemeal flour are good, but 85% flour is probably the best general base.

125 g (4 oz) rice
15 g ($\frac{1}{2}$ oz) fresh yeast or
  $\frac{1}{2}$ as much dried yeast
scant 25 g (1 oz) salt
450 g (1 lb) flour

Simmer the rice in plenty of water until it is just tender. Drain, reserving the liquid. Cool the rice and rice water; add some of the rice water to the yeast, and a pinch of sugar if using dried yeast. Add the rice and salt to the warmed flour, mix in the yeast liquid, then add enough of the tepid rice water to make a smooth, pliable dough. Knead lightly for a few minutes, then let rise. Shape, prove and bake at 205°C, 400°F/Gas 6. Timings vary considerably so watch closely, turning the heat down a little after 30 minutes.

Corn-meal hushpuppies

Bread made with a large proportion of corn meal is soft and needs to be eaten straight from the baking pan (hence spoon bread, see p.48). These rolls from the southern USA are firmer in texture than corn-meal bread but also need to be enjoyed hot because they are fried, not baked.

50 g (2 oz) strong white flour
15 g ($\frac{1}{2}$ oz) baking powder
15 g ($\frac{1}{2}$ oz) sugar
pinch salt
175 g (6 oz) yellow corn
   meal
1 beaten egg
175 ml (6 fl oz) milk
finely chopped small onion
   (optional)

Combine dry ingredients, add egg and milk and stir lightly. Add onion, if using.

Fry a few rolls at a time, dropping the dough from a teaspoon. Use either a frying-pan or a deep-fryer; the oil should be heated until just smoking. Drain on absorbent paper and keep hot.

Potato bread

There are very few rules about potato breads, except that almost none uses potato flour. Potato does make bread of excellent keeping qualities, which is why the old homemade leavens and yeasts always included po-tatoes, or potato water. Either use potato water to mix, or add a small amount of potato to a large amount of wheat flour, or make bread with almost all potato, ac-cording to taste (a mid-course is more usual).

For every 450 g (1 lb) flour, preferably white, use 125 g (4 oz) potato, weighed after the following process.

Cook the potatoes in their skins until really soft right through. Drain, chop rough-ly, then place over a very low heat to steam dry (covering with a cloth will help). Sieve the potatoes, weigh them and use them warm.

Two fairly large potatoes should weigh about 125 g (4 oz) after cooking and draining, but the weight is not critical.

Use lukewarm scalded milk, plenty of salt and the normal amount of yeast:

15 g ($\frac{1}{2}$ oz) for up to
   1 kg (2 lb) mixture, 25 g
   (1 oz) for anything over

Providing the potatoes have been dried thoroughly, they can even be used in equal proportions to the flour.

Barley bread

It is not easy to find barley flour or meal today. It may even be necessary to buy it from an animal-foodstuff supplier, sorting out the coarse bran yourself. How-ever, barley flour does make wonderful bread and is worth the trouble. The best plan for barley flour is to make a sour-dough base from it and use this to leaven bread made of white or 85% flour (see sour-dough section, pp. 44-6). A little butter or creamy milk should be used when mixing the bread.

Rye breads

This book contains several recipes, of a specialized kind, for rye bread. Other-wise, if you replace up to one-fifth of your normal flour with light rye flour you will have a delicious loaf that keeps astonishingly well. Greater proportions than one-fifth need careful hand-ling, for the bread tends to lose its shape during baking.

Wheatgerm bread

It is foolish to consider putting wheatgerm back into white flour; use whole-meal flour instead. How-ever, if you want to enrich bread with the vitamins of wheatgerm, use up to 50 g (2 oz) per ·5 kg (1 lb) flour. Some cooks sprinkle wheat-germ on to the sides and bottom of their loaf tins.

Oatmeal bread

Oatmeal is another grain that is successful as an additive but not as the sole constituent of bread. Sub-stitute up to one-fifth of your normal flour or 85% flour (the latter is probably best). Oatmeal is fatty itself, but responds well when there is a small proportion of milk or butter in the dough.

▶ Clockwise from top right: French sticks; savoury wholemeal with ham and olives; flowerpot wholemeal; white pitta, stuffed pitta; sweet white plait with mixed fruit and pineapple chunks; bagels filled with smoked salmon and cream cheese; savoury wholemeal plait with chopped onion and cheese; 85%-flour khachapuri (p. 70) filled with cheese flavoured with tomato purée, garlic and oregano.

Enriched breads

The additives which enrich the flavour and vitamin or mineral content of bread often improve keeping quality, too. Milk, eggs, butter and cooking fats are the most common additions. Excellent results are easily obtained by experimenting with soya flour, oats, bran, wheatgerm, molasses, honey, syrup, fruit juice and fruit or vegetable purées. There are few rules and common sense is usually enough to prevent major disasters. The recipe for 'good health' bread gives a good guide to the usual proportions of some of the most commonly used enrichers.

Good health bread

25 g (1 oz) fresh yeast
675 ml (24 fl oz) warm water
25 g (1 oz) honey
350 g (12 oz) wholemeal flour
25 g (1 oz) sea salt
50 g (2 oz) wheatgerm
50 g (2 oz) soya flour
25 g (1 oz) non-fat milk powder
25 ml (1 fl oz) oil or melted butter
350 g (12 oz) strong white flour

Activate the yeast in some of the warm water, adding a pinch of sugar if using dried yeast. Dissolve the honey in the rest of the water and combine the two liquids. Add the wholemeal flour. Beat well with a wooden spoon, gradually adding all other ingredients except the white flour.

When mixed, slowly incorporate the white flour. It should become relatively stiff; you may have to add up to 50 g (2 oz) more flour.

Turn out the dough and knead until smooth and elastic. Place in a warmed oiled bowl and cover with a damp cloth. When doubled in size, punch down and knead lightly. Divide into two pieces, shape into loaves and put into greased bread tins. Allow to raise again until just over the top of the tin. Bake for 50-60 minutes at 170°C, 325°F/Gas 3. The bread shrinks a little in cooking, so you may not need to finish baking them out of their tins.

Variations All white flour can be used for a lighter, slightly bigger loaf.

Vienna bread

This is quite unusual if authentic. For domestic purposes, a good Vienna-style loaf can be made simply by mixing a white-flour dough with milk. It is usual to sprinkle Viennas with poppy seeds.

Chollah

Traditionally associated with Jewish festivals, this is a semi-sweet, plaited loaf, sometimes made with milk, sometimes eggs, sometimes both. Make a dough of 1·5 kg (about 3 lb) strong white flour, add 4 eggs and up to 225 g (8 oz) sugar. Mix with milk or water. The dough needs good kneading and two risings. Proportions of egg, milk and sugar are infinitely variable; but do not

add too much sugar at the start.

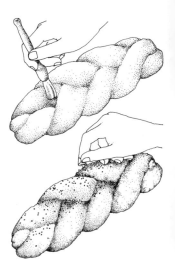

Bagels

These traditional Jewish rolls are especially popular in New York as 'lox and bagel' (smoked salmon and cream cheese on a hot bagel).

275 ml (10 fl oz) milk or water
15 g ($\frac{1}{2}$ oz) fresh yeast or $\frac{1}{2}$ as much dried yeast
25 g (1 oz sugar)
5 g (1 teaspoon) salt
50 g (2 oz) margarine, butter or oil
1 egg white (optional)
1 egg yolk
450 g (1 lb) strong white flour

Warm the milk or water and cream the yeast with some of it, adding a pinch of the sugar if using dried yeast. Meanwhile, dissolve the sugar and salt and melt the butter or margarine in the rest of the liquid. When just lukewarm, add the creamed yeast. If using,

beat the egg white stiffly and add to the liquid. Beat the egg yolk, add to the liquid and mix the liquid into the flour.

Knead until smooth: the dough will be firmer than the average bread dough. When the dough just begins to rise (after an hour at the most), knead lightly, pull off small pieces, roll to about the width of a finger and form into rings.

Leave again until just starting to rise—10-15 minutes.

Drop the bagels, one or two at a time, into a large saucepan full of water that is just simmering. Cook until the bagels rise to the surface. Remove with a slotted spatula or kitchen tongs.

Place on greased baking trays. Bake at 205°C, 400°F/ Gas 6 for about 15 minutes. Serve warm.

Variations Bagels can be sprinkled with caraway, salt, poppy seeds or, traditionally, sesame seeds. Seasoned or garlic salt can be added instead.

Fruited and spiced breads

Sweet breads were once simply part of the week's basic dough that had fruit, spice and perhaps a little milk or butter worked into it. Now, they are often made specially, but if you make a lot of bread it is worth saving a little dough—either whole-meal, 85% or white—for the purpose of making these delicious breads. There is almost no end to the variety of fruits and spices that can be added: chopped dried apricots, chopped stem ginger, grated orange peel with mixed spice, ground carda-mom or cinnamon, chopped dates and walnuts and coco-nut are just a few. Ground cumin and coriander pro-duce a most fragrant bread. Fruit juices and fruit purées can be substituted for milk or water as liquids for mixing.

Raisin and malt loaf
125 g (4 oz) raisins
225 g (8 oz) 85% flour
pinch salt
25 g (1 oz) fresh yeast or
$\frac{1}{2}$ as much dried yeast
25 g (1 oz) butter
25 ml (1 fl oz) molasses
50 ml (2 fl oz) malt extract
warm water or milk
225 g (8 oz) 85% flour
5 g (1 teaspoon) mixed
spice

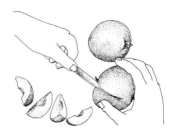

Toss the raisins in the flour and salt. Activate the yeast. Melt the butter, molasses and malt. Cool. Mix the ingredients with milk or water and flour to form soft dough. Knead, prove, knead lightly; prove again in loaf tin. Bake at 205°C, 400°F/ Gas 6 for 40-45 minutes. Glaze with honey.

Kentucky apple bread
This American recipe uses baking soda, but you could substitute 15 g ($\frac{1}{2}$ oz) fresh yeast or $\frac{1}{2}$ as much dried yeast.
125 g (4 oz) softened butter
125 g (4 oz) sugar
2 eggs
250 g (8 oz) white flour
pinch salt
10 g ($\frac{1}{2}$ oz) baking soda
25 ml (1 fl oz) buttermilk
5 ml (1 teaspoon) vanilla
extract
250 g (8 oz) apples, peeled
and cored
Cream the butter and sugar. Beat in the eggs thoroughly, one at a time. Stir in the flour and salt. Dissolve the soda in the buttermilk, then mix in well. Add the vanilla extract and the apples, finely chopped and sprinkled with lemon juice. Spoon into a small greased and floured loaf tin.

Cover with a topping made from equal portions of butter, sugar and flour (about 50 g/2 oz of each) mixed to the consistency of bread-crumbs and flavoured with cinnamon (about 5 g/1 teaspoon). Sprinkle over the loaf and bake at 165°C, 325°F/Gas 3 for at least 1 hour.

Variations Failing butter-milk, substitute sweet milk and use 15 g ($\frac{1}{2}$ oz) baking powder instead of the soda.

Spices such as nutmeg or mace are excellent in this bread—but always include cinnamon in the topping. Chopped walnuts, dates and even peanut butter can be added too. Crunchy toppings are typical of fruit breads and German streusels.

Fresh fruit loaf

This marvellous pudding or tea-time treat can be made with some leftover dough and almost any fruit you have in stock. You can make one or two little loaves or use the full quantities of a dough recipe to make several larger ones for slicing. Roll or stretch the dough to about ·5 cm ($\frac{1}{4}$ in) thick, in as square a shape as possible.

Spread the sliced fruit down the middle third (use apples, peaches, bananas and raisins, apricots, soft fruits such as blackberries, currants or raspberries, pears with a little ginger, and so on). Slice the remaining thirds as shown (like Danish pastry mock plait). Sprinkle brown sugar and spices over the whole, together with a little rum or liqueur if de-

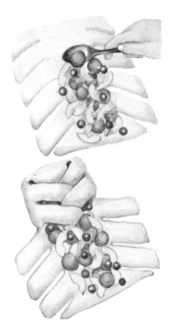

sired. Fold in the flaps to form a tight loaf.

Leave to rise just 20-30 minutes, then bake at 180°C, 350°F/Gas 4 for about 1 hour.

Variations These are limit-less: you can spice up the dough or add fruit to it. Currants, peel and mixed spice in the dough and apples in the centre would make a superb winter's pudding to eat with cream or custard.

The top can be glazed, sprinkled with sugar, scattered with nuts and currants or further decorated by snipping and cutting with scissors or a sharp knife before baking.

Soaked dried fruit can be used and, whether dried or fresh, the fruit will be especially good if placed on a bed of thick custard.

Savoury breads

A savoury bread is usually a basic dough to which cheese, vegetables or herbs have been added. The varieties are countless. Different combinations of herbs, vegetable juices (tomato, carrot, etc.), onion, garlic and grated vegetables produce endless permutations.

Cheese breads can include nutmeg, herbs or vegetables. There are also beer breads, which tend to be better if a dark brew is used in combination with whole-meal or rye flour.

The following ideas are for a dough made of 1·5 kg (3 lb) flour. Any of the following asterisked ingredients or mixtures can be mixed into the flour or spread on the flattened dough and rolled up in it.
*1 minced onion and 15 g ($\frac{1}{2}$ oz) dill weed
*1 minced onion, clove of garlic, minced parsley
*225 g (8 oz) grated cheese (more if a mild cheese)
*cheese with chopped chives or cheese, chives and garlic or cheese and curry powder
*25 g (1 oz) mixed or Italian dried herbs
*225-350 g (8-12 oz) grated carrots, mixed with nutmeg and orange juice and/or grated orange peel
Liquid additives include stock made with a chicken stock cube and herbs or tomato juice (or thinned tomato purée), possibly spiked with Worcestershire sauce.

Pastries and brioches

For sophisticated entertaining, nothing matches fragrant yeasted pastries and sponges: hot croissants straight from the oven on a lazy Sunday; petits pains au chocolat for a self-indulgent tea; colourful Danish pastries at any time. All are much simpler to make than anyone would guess.

Croissants

25 g (1 oz) fresh yeast or
  $\frac{1}{2}$ as much dried yeast
25 g (1 oz) butter or lard
5 g (1 teaspoon) salt
15 g (1 tablespoon) sugar*
150 ml (5 fl oz) lukewarm,
  scalded milk
350 g (12 oz) strong white
  flour
125 g (4 oz) butter
egg and milk for glaze

Activate the yeast in a little warm water, adding a pinch of sugar if using dried yeast. Meanwhile, dissolve the sugar and salt and melt the first quantity of butter (or lard) in the scalded milk. Add the yeast. Work in the flour, then knead thoroughly until the dough is really smooth and supple. Leave to rise, covered, until doubled in size.

Knock the dough down, then chill.

Roll out the dough on a floured board to make a strip three times longer than it is wide. Chill the butter well, then either flake it and arrange it evenly down the centre of the dough (if following the simple method), or flake one-third of the butter over two-thirds of the dough (alternative method).

Simple method Continue by folding one-third of the dough into the centre and

folding the other third over that.

Give it a half turn, roll out to the original size, then chill for 10-15 minutes. Fold, turn, roll and chill at least twice more. Chill thoroughly before proceeding.

Alternative method Fold the dough into thirds, folding in the unbuttered third first. Give it a half turn and roll out to the previous size.

Chill for 10-15 minutes. Then butter, fold, turn and roll again. Chill, then repeat.

After this third chilling, fold, turn and roll the dough at least three more times, but without adding more butter and without chilling between times. At the end of this process, chill the dough once more.

Finishing The croissant dough can now be treated in various ways. It can be wrapped and frozen, or the croissants can be made up then left in the refrigerator overnight.

When shaping the croissants, work as fast as you can and in reasonably cool surroundings: a warm kitchen will melt the butter and make the desired flakiness impossible. Divide the dough in half, roll each half into an even strip or a circle and cut out triangle shapes with a base of about 15 cm (6 in).

Starting at the base, roll up each triangle loosely, finally tucking the tip under.

Curve the rolls into a crescent shape. Space out on a greased baking tray.

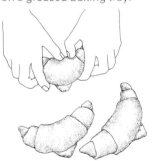

Now either put the croissants into the refrigerator overnight to rise slowly, letting them return to room temperature before baking, or let them prove in a warm place for 20-30 minutes, then chill them for just 10 minutes to ensure butter is set.

Brush the croissants with lightly beaten egg and bake at 220°C, 425°F/Gas 7 for 15-20 minutes.

Danish pastries

These were supposedly invented in Vienna, but are now a Scandinavian speciality.

225 g (8 oz) strong white flour
pinch salt
15 g (½ oz) sugar
2-3 g (½ teaspoon) ground cardamom
15 g (½ oz) fresh yeast or ½ as much dried yeast
125 ml (4 fl oz) milk or milk and water mixed
1 egg
125 g (4 oz) butter

Sift the flour, salt, sugar and cardamom into a bowl. Warm a little of the milk and activate the yeast in it. When creamy, add to the rest of the (cold) milk, mix in the beaten egg, then work into the flour to make a dough. Knead until satin-smooth. Chill for 10-15 minutes. Roll out to a square about 1 cm (½ in) thick on a lightly floured board.

Chill the butter and cut it into thin, even slices. Place these side by side down the centre of the pastry (not right to the edges).

Either fold the unbuttered thirds over the butter, so they lie on top of one another, or fold them into the centre so they just touch (the first way is the easier).

Seal all round with a rolling pin, give the pastry a half turn, roll out to about its original size, then chill for 15 minutes.

Now fold, turn, roll, fold and rest twice more.

Note All fillings should be prepared before (or during, if necessary) the pastry-making, as no long proving is required.

Fillings Although many fruit purées and canned or dried fruits such as apricots and pineapple will withstand the very hot oven temperatures necessary, the most popular Scandinavian fillings are those described below.

Almond filling Mix together equal quantities of finely chopped, blanched almonds (or crushed macaroons), butter and castor sugar until even and smooth. Add a little cinnamon or orange juice if desired.

Butter filling Cream together equal quantities of unsalted butter and icing sugar, then add currants for a really firm texture.

Custard filling Use a little leftover custard made with a commercial powder, or make up a small quantity following the instructions on the packet. If liked, add a few drops of vanilla essence, mix in some ground almonds or apple purée.

Dried-fruit fillings Cook chopped dates, raisins, candied peel, prunes, apricots (and so on; or just use two or three of these) to a pulp in lemon or orange juice and honey, flavoured with cinnamon, brown sugar and rum. Mincemeat will of course suit admirably.

Larger dried fruits, such as apricots, peaches and apple rings, should be soaked until just tender before cooking. Drained canned fruits can also be used. Both are better with lemon juice.

Honey filling Honey is best mixed with nuts, either ground or finely chopped.

Icing Water icing is always used for Danish pastries. It can be flavoured with fruit juice or, traditionally, with rum. The icing should be thin. Different effects can be created by icing some pastries when hot, which makes the icing transparent, and some cold, when it becomes opaque.

Danish pastry shapes
Squares, stars or circles cut with pastry cutters make delightful small pastries, simply glazed. With or without filling, all pastries should prove on a baking tray for 15 minutes then cook for about 15 minutes at 230°C, 450°F/Gas 8. Best icing effects are achieved by dribbling water icing on top when the pastries are hot and again, later, when they are cold.

Snails Spread the dough with butter filling, sprinkle with cinnamon, roll tightly and cut into slices. Dot the centres with icing when cold.

Pinwheels Cut right through the roll (see *Snails*) at each third cut. Spread the joined pinwheels slightly. Alternatively, do not cut right through, but spread into one big wheel. Ice when hot.

Pastry crown Double the quantities in the recipe on p. 63, including that of yeast. Line a ring mould with half the mixture; make snails with variety of fillings with the remaining mixture. Arrange the snails evenly. When cooked, glaze with melted apricot jam; ice with rum water icing when cold.

Mock plait Cut large or small squares of pastry dough as shown. Spread the fruit filling down the centre, then overlap the flaps as shown. Brush with egg and sprinkle with flaked almonds.

Coxcombs Put almond filling or apple purée along the centre of squares of pastry. Fold, seal and cut into desired length. Cut the sealed edge several times, bend outwards. Glaze and scatter with crushed sugar cubes.

Dragon's teeth Begin as for coxcombs. Make many cuts, starting from the folded edge; break through only at the sealed edge. Twist to open the cuts, glaze and sprinkle with nuts.

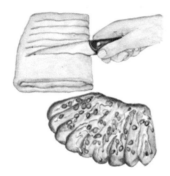

Windmills Cut and fold squares as shown. Put almond filling in the centre of each square.

Birthday pretzel Roll out a double quantity of pastry (see recipe, p. 63) to only 7·5-10 cm (3-4 in) wide. Spread the centre with almond or varied fillings. Turn the outer edges in but do not join them.

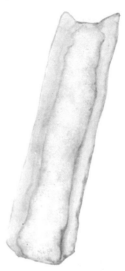

Envelopes Start with squares. Blob jam or custard in the centre of each. Fold in the corners; top each envelope with a cherry.

To vary, fold in only one, two or three corners; or try adding different fillings at either end, folding in the two opposite corners.

Pastry plait Either cut, fill and roll three stuffed strands of pastry and plait these; or sprinkle in fruit and spice as you plait flat strips.

Shape as shown below. When proved, glaze and sprinkle with almonds and crushed sugar cubes. Bake for 20 minutes.

Children would be delighted to be given a birthday pretzel topped with candles.

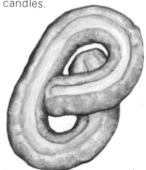

Brioches

Strictly speaking, most plain or lightly-flavoured sweet yeasted cakes can be regarded as brioches, whatever their provenance. Brioche dough is a survivor from the time when all cakes that did not include eggs were leavened with yeast.

The plain brioche now associated with France is clearly the ancestor of our modern sponge and first cousin to Italian *pannetone,* German *Gugelhopf,* Polish *babke* and so on. Brioches are usually eaten at breakfast- or coffee-time.

Brioches are best eaten hot, sweet and steaming from the oven. The accompanying heady smell of yeast should never be detected on the tongue. Brioches will also re-heat quite well.

There are many, many brioche recipes, the proportions of milk, water, eggs and butter being the variable element. The recipe that follows is fairly typical. Brioches can be baked with or without a topknot, in one large or several small moulds. *Makes up to 12 small brioches*

25 g (1 oz) fresh yeast or ½ as much dried yeast

25 ml (1 fl oz) lukewarm milk, previously scalded

225 g (8 oz) strong white flour

pinch salt

15 g (½ oz) sugar

2 eggs

125 g (4 oz) unsalted butter

Oil the brioche mould or moulds. Activate the yeast in the milk, adding a pinch of the sugar if using dried yeast.

Sift the flour, salt and sugar. Mix in the yeast, beaten eggs and melted butter well. Beat with a wooden spoon. Knead for about 5 minutes or until really smooth and supple. Leave to rise, covered, until doubled in size. Knead lightly for 1 minute.

Leave the dough in a cool place overnight.

Next morning, handle the dough very lightly or the brioches will not be as airy as they should be.

If making small brioches, roll the dough out lightly into a sausage and cut into as many pieces as required. Either fill the oiled moulds or, for small brioches with topknots, use three-quarters of each piece of dough to half-fill the moulds, then poke a floured finger into each, roll the remaining

quarters of dough and plug them firmly into the holes.

Otherwise, for one large brioche, put all the dough into a large fluted mould. Leave to rise in a relatively cool place until the dough is light and puffy and just below the top of the moulds.

Bake at 230°C, 450°F/ Gas 8 for 10 minutes (small) or 20-25 minutes (large).

The larger brioches are often more successful if a sharp knife is run round the centre just before baking. This allows the dough to rise through the middle and gives a soufflé-like type of cap. Brioches may be glazed, either with beaten egg just before baking or with a sugar glaze just before they are fully cooked—a few spoons of milk and sugar boiled together for a couple of minutes is sufficient.

Variations A small amount of lemon juice makes brioches more suitable for teatime consumption. Adding a little mixed peel with raisins and currants will produce something closer to Italian *pannetone,* usually made at Christmas.

Sausage in brioche

This is a classic recipe now rarely found on restaurant menus. Provided suitable sausage is available, it is a novel idea for a lunch at home or a good savoury starter for a dinner party. The type of sausage used should be the type normally sold as a boiling sausage and should be totally free from any bread or cereal filling. The texture should be coarse, and a smoky or garlic flavour would be an added advantage. Delicatessens selling Polish sausages are likely to stock reasonably-priced sausages of this type —choose mazurska or a piece of boiling ring. Pure pork Italian and French sausages are more expensive but more authentic; German bratwurst would be excellent.

Traditionally the sausages for this dish would weigh about 500 g (about 1 lb) but there is no reason why several smaller sausages cannot be used. As the brioche dough has to be shaped around the sausage the dough must be firmer than that for cooking in a mould. Make up the recipe on p. 66, using only 5 g (1 teaspoon) sugar and up to 350 g (12 oz) strong white flour.

Follow the directions, kneading rather than mixing or beating where these instructions are indicated. Cook the sausage so that it is ready when the dough is proven. Wrap the sausage or sausages in dough while still warm, making a good seal. Glaze with a little beaten egg or cream. Leave for 15 minutes in a warm place, then bake at 220°C, 425°F/Gas 7 for 20-25 minutes.

Slide from the baking tray on to a folded white napkin on a heated serving dish and slice it at the table.

Frankfurter brioche

If you have not been successful in obtaining the right

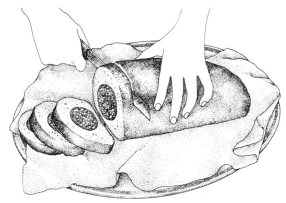

type of sausage for the preceding recipe, try this.

Follow the above directions but make individual rolls by rolling the dough into rectangles about 5 mm ($\frac{1}{4}$ in) thick, each just big enough to wrap once around a frankfurter.

Seal well, leave to prove for 10 minutes on a baking sheet, glaze with egg or cream, then bake for 10-15 minutes at 220°C, 425°F/Gas 7.

The frankfurters can be split and smeared with mustard before they are wrapped in the brioche dough.

Croissants jambons

These make sophisticated and filling breakfast fare for leisurely weekend mornings. Simply make croissant dough (see p. 62) using only 5 g (1 teaspoon) of the sugar.

When ready to roll up the croissants, lay a good, thick slice of smoked ham on the dough and roll the croissant around this. Then prove and bake in the normal way.

If you want to use bacon, cook it first and trim off the

excess fat. Of course, savoury croissants can be made with an infinite variety of the fillings; for example, use a cream cheese flavoured with fresh herbs or chop up some cold, creamy scrambled egg with a little smoked salmon.

Petits pains au chocolat

These are the ultimate self-indulgent luxury for memorable breakfasts or elegant teas.

Brioche, croissant or enriched bread dough can be used, but the first two tend to be too rich when accompanied by rich, melted dark chocolate. It is therefore best to use a simple bread dough made with milk rather than water.

To make each petit pain, divide the dough into portions weighing up to 50 g (2 oz) and shape each into a rectangle. Place 15 g ($\frac{1}{2}$ oz) dark chocolate on each. Fold the dough to make a neat package. Leave for 15 minutes to prove, glaze with egg or cream, then bake at 220°C, 425°F/Gas 7 for 15 minutes. Eat while still hot.

Inter-national yeast cookery

Yeast means treats wherever you are in the world. From satisfying rounds of Italian pizza to honey-saturated Arabic delights and traditional English buns, dough appears in every possible guise—with nuts, sprinkled with rose water, stuffed with jam, baked, fried, moulded, beaten, and twisted—and is universally consumed with pleasure.

Pissaladière

This is an oniony, salty sort of pizza from France.

900 g (2 lb) onions
140 ml (5 fl oz) rich olive oil
450 g (1 lb) white bread dough, once risen *or* pizza mixture (see below)
20 pitted black olives
12 anchovy fillets

Slice the onions finely and cook in the oil over a low heat until they are soft.

Pull or roll out the dough to about 1 cm ($\frac{1}{2}$ in) thick; place on a baking tray. Then cover with the onion. Decorate with the olives and anchovies, then bake in a moderate oven for 30 minutes. Serve with a crisp green salad.

Variations Use unsweetened pastry instead of dough. Or use 2-3-cm (1-in) slices of bread, cut lengthwise from a loaf. Fry on one side in butter or oil, coat the other with the cooked onions, olives and anchovies and bake for 10 minutes only.

Pizza

Often misunderstood and misrepresented, the pizza is now irreplaceable. Commercial pizzas have become savoury tarts on a biscuit-like base. Others are merely repositories for leftovers.

True pizza has a light, milk-dough base, cooked to a slight crispness round the edge. The toppings are simple but rich and should always blend into the dough rather than curling and crisping on top.

Some of the modern inventions are truly delicious. But none is more so than the original.

For the base of a pizza to serve 3-4 people, use white bread dough (p. 52) made from about 225 g (8 oz) flour, 25 g (1 oz) yeast (or $\frac{1}{2}$ as much dried yeast), some warm milk and an egg (you can use just water, but the dough won't re-heat so well). Ideally, take a little less than 450 g (1 lb) white bread dough from a batch you are already making. Knead well and leave to rise in a warm place until doubled in size.

Gently fry two large onions and some garlic in good olive oil until they are soft and mushy. Add about 450 g (1 lb or so) fresh tomatoes, or the equivalent of canned tomatoes, drained. Sprinkle in oreganum, cook for a minute or so, then leave to cool.

Using a rolling pin and your fingertips, roll and stretch the dough into a circle or square on a greased baking tray. It should be about 1 cm ($\frac{1}{2}$ in) thick.

Spread the tomato mixture evenly, almost to the edge. Then decorate with anchovy fillets and small black olives. Leave for 10 minutes or until the dough just starts to rise, then cook at 220°C, 425°F/Gas 7 for 15-20 minutes. Eat straight away.

Variations Leave out the onion and garlic altogether. Drained, canned plum tomatoes, gently squeezed between the fingers, make an excellent base; sprinkle generously with oreganum. Cheese has become a popular pizza ingredient: almost any hard variety can be used; strong Cheddar is good. The anchovy fillets and olives should be put on top of the cheese, sliced or grated.

Slices of salami and mozzarella, green or hot peppers, gherkins, baby clams, prawn, chorizo or chopped ham can all be used for pizza toppings.

Large pizzas benefit from being sprinkled with oil before being put in the oven.

▶ This 'modern' pizza oven is like the old bread ovens.

Yachtsman's bread

This is a curiosity from New Zealand, but practical nonetheless.

15 g ($\frac{1}{2}$ oz) dried yeast
350 ml (12 fl oz) sea water*
15 g ($\frac{1}{2}$ oz) sugar
450 g (1 lb) strong white flour

*not recommended in the Mediterranean or any other area where pollution is suspected!

Activate the yeast with a little water and a pinch of sugar. When frothy, stir in the remaining water then mix in the flour. Kneading is not necessary. Put the dough into a well greased and floured pressure cooker or heavy saucepan with a tight-fitting lid. Leave to rise with the lid on for 2 hours or so in medium warmth. Cook over a low flame on top of the stove for 30 minutes. Then turn the loaf over in the pan and cook for another 30 minutes.

Swedish rusks

This is a savoury standby for drinks or soups.

50 g (2 oz) fresh yeast or $\frac{1}{2}$ as much dried yeast
40 g (1$\frac{1}{2}$ oz) sugar
675 g (24 fl oz) sour milk
500 g (just over 1 lb) rye flour, coarse if possible
5 g (1 level teaspoon) salt
85 g (3 oz) lard
flavourings: fennel seed, aniseed, cardamom, dill

Activate the yeast with a little milk and, if using dried yeast, a pinch of sugar. Add the milk, lukewarm. Mix in the rye flour and salt, then the melted fat (not too hot). Add in flavourings while kneading lightly and briefly. Roll into long thin strands, using wholemeal rather than rye flour on the work surface. Place on a greased baking sheet, prick,

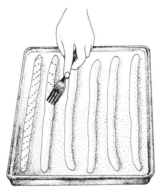

and leave to rise. Bake at 180°C, 350°F/Gas 4 for 15 minutes.

When cool, cut into smaller pieces and dry these in a warm oven. Keep in an airtight tin.

Khachapuri (see p. 57)

For authenticity, use freshly-made sheep's cheese for this Russian bread. Otherwise, soft goat's cheese or curd cheese will do.

15 g ($\frac{1}{2}$ oz) fresh yeast or $\frac{1}{2}$ as much dried yeast
80 ml (just under 3 fl oz) lukewarm, scalded milk
1 egg
25 g (1 oz) sugar
pinch salt
450 g (1 lb) strong white flour
50 g (2 oz) melted butter
1 egg
175 g (6 oz) soft cheese

Activate the yeast in some of the warm milk adding a pinch of sugar if using dried yeast. When frothy, add the beaten egg, sugar and pinch of salt.

Mix into a firm dough with the flour, then add the warm melted butter. Now either continue as below or knead and prove the dough before doing so.

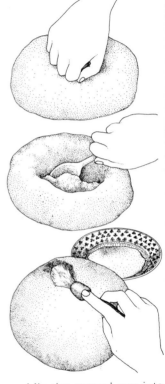

Mix the second egg into the cheese. Shape the dough into a ball, punch down the centre and put the cheese in this. Re-shape around the cheese, pinch the edges together and glaze with a little beaten egg.

Let it begin to rise, covered, then bake at 205°C, 400°F/Gas 6 for 35-40 minutes. Rub over with butter after removing from the oven.

Variations These are infinite. Sweeten the cheese, and add spice to the dough. Add fresh herbs to the cheese, especially chopped fresh mint or garlic. Mix fruit, such as drained crushed pineapple or apple purée, into the cheese.

Pahlava (see p. 73)

(see p. 73)

This recipe, from Georgia, USSR, is a yeasted version of baklava, which is made in Greece and Turkey with flaky phyllo pastry. Pahlava may indeed be the original recipe.

10 g ($\frac{1}{3}$ oz) fresh yeast or $\frac{1}{2}$
   as much dried yeast
70 ml (scant 3 fl oz)
   full-cream milk
1 egg
5 g (1 teaspoon) salt
225 g (8 oz) strong white
   flour
50 g (2 oz) melted butter
125 g (4 oz) ground
   almonds or walnuts, or a
   mixture of both
125 g (4 oz) sugar
honey
saffron
egg yolk

Activate the yeast in a little of the milk, adding a pinch of the sugar if using dried yeast. When it is frothy, add in the rest of the milk, the beaten egg and the salt. Make a dough with this liquid and the flour, then mix in the warm, melted butter. Cover. Leave to rise for about $1\frac{1}{2}$ hours.

Roll out the dough on a lightly floured board until it is *extremely* thin. Oil or grease a baking tray. Cut the dough into strips, large or small as preferred.

Put one strip on the sheet; cover with a layer of ground nuts and sugar, bound together with a little honey. Then add a second layer of dough. Continue until all the dough and the stuffing are used up.

Using a very sharp knife, cut the pahlava into triangles or diamonds. Separate slightly.

Mix an egg yolk with a good pinch of ground saffron and smear this over the tops. Put half a walnut or almond on top of each.

Leave until just beginning to rise, then bake at 180°-200°C, 350°-400°F/Gas 4-6 for 35-40 minutes (use the lower temperature for small ones). Half-way through cooking, pour hot honey over the pahlava and return to the oven. Sprinkle some chopped pistachios over the top for added colour, or mix into the stuffing with ground almonds.

Savarin

Savarin is a simple but exotic end to a meal.
Batter:
  25 g (1 oz) fresh yeast or
   $\frac{1}{2}$ as much dried yeast
  50 ml (2 fl oz) warm,
   scalded milk
  2 eggs
  pinch salt
  5 g (1 teaspoon) sugar
  50 g (2 oz) butter
  125 g (4 oz) strong white
   flour
Syrup:
  80 g (3 oz) sugar
  450 ml (16 fl oz) water
  liqueur

Activate the yeast in the warm milk, adding a pinch of sugar if using dried yeast. When it is working well, beat in the eggs, salt and sugar, then the butter, which must be only just melted. Pour gradually into the flour, beating with a wooden spoon all the time; aim for a thick batter rather than a dough.

Butter a ring mould, half-fill, cover and leave until doubled in size. Bake at 205°C, 400°F/Gas 6 for 20-25 minutes. Meanwhile, prepare the syrup by boiling together the sugar and water for just 1 minute. Flavour the liquid with liqueur: for a fruit-filled savarin, kirsch or Cointreau; for one to be served simply with its syrup and cream, rum or a strong, sharp liqueur, such as Poire Williams.

As soon as the savarin is a rich golden brown, remove from the oven and from the mould, put it on a wire tray resting on a dish and gently prick it with a fine fork or skewer. Pour over the lukewarm syrup, spooning it back again and again so that the excess is soaked up. Savarin may be decorated with almonds and cherries but is usually served plain.

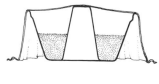

Rum babas

Use the recipe for savarin on p. 71, but bake for 15 minutes in small ring moulds, include a handful of currants, and use rum, of course, to flavour the syrup.

Note If doubling the recipe quantities, do not increase the amount of yeast.

Loukoumades

These are small, honeyed doughnuts from the Greek islands.

50 g (2 oz) fresh yeast or
  ½ as much dried yeast
250 g (8 oz) strong white
  flour
5 g (1 level teaspoon) salt
lukewarm water
oil
honey
sugar
cinnamon

Activate the yeast in a little lukewarm water, adding a pinch of sugar if using dried yeast. Make a well in the flour, add the salt and yeast, then work in enough luke-warm water to make a dough that will drop easily from a spoon. Leave covered in a basin until it starts bubbling. In a deep sauce-pan, heat 7-10 cm (3-4 in) of good oil. When the oil starts to haze, drop the dough in from a spoon and fry to a golden colour. Dip-ping the spoon into a cup of cold water will prevent the dough sticking to it.

Drain the loukoumades on absorbent paper and keep warm.

Pile on a platter, pour on some warmed clear honey, some sugar and then a dusting of ground cinnamon.

Oliebollen

These fruit-filled Dutch doughnuts are traditionally made for New Year's Eve but are wonderful on any cold winter's night.

50 g (1 oz) fresh yeast or
  ½ as much dried yeast
175 ml (6 fl oz) lukewarm,
  scalded milk
1 lemon
1 large cooking apple
1 egg
50 g (2 oz) raisins
25 g (1 oz) chopped peel
225 g (8 oz) strong white
  flour
pinch salt
castor or icing sugar

Activate the yeast in some of the warm milk, adding a pinch of sugar if using dried yeast. Grate the peel of half the lemon. Squeeze the le-mon and grate the peeled apple into the juice. Add this to the lemon and yeast mixtures together with the rest of the ingredients, except the sugar, and mix well. Cover with a damp cloth and leave to rise for 1 hour.

Knock down and knead very lightly a few times. Then shape the doughnuts, either by using two oiled spoons or by rolling in your palms. Let the doughnuts recover and begin to rise, then drop them into deep, very hot oil, a few at a time.

When puffed and golden, drain on absorbent paper. Roll in castor sugar or icing sugar. Serve warm.

Variations Knead the dough really well before adding the fruit. This will give rather lighter results.

A little cinnamon can also be added.

Clockwise, from top right: Moroccan griouches, Berliner kranzküchen, Moroccan chebbakia, English Chelsea buns, Russian pahlava, Polish poppy-seed loaf.

Jam doughnuts

Almost every European country claims to have a version of its own. Use the basic dough from oliebollen (yeast, milk, flour and salt) but add in 25 g (1 oz) sugar.

After knocking down the risen dough, make balls either by using two oiled spoons or by rolling pieces of dough in your palms. Flatten with a rolling pin. Drop 5 ml (1 teaspoon) jam (ideally, raspberry) on the middle of each piece of dough, then re-seal the

doughnuts with a dab of milk and re-shape.

Set to rise for about 15 minutes before cooking in deep, hot oil. Then sprinkle with sugar.

If you are not going to eat them straight away, try coating them, as they do in Poland, in a thin icing made with just icing sugar and water while still warm.

Variations A good dash of rum can be added to the mixture. Apricot jam can be added, and a sprinkling of cinnamon sugar.

Semolina ghoriba

This popular macaroon-like biscuit is from Morocco.

15 g ($\frac{1}{2}$ oz) fresh yeast or
  $\frac{1}{2}$ as much dried yeast
3 eggs
225 g (8 oz) sugar
50 ml (2 fl oz) peanut oil
50 g (2 oz) melted butter
few drops vanilla essence
450 g (1 lb) fine semolina
orange-flower water

Activate the yeast in a little warm water, adding a pinch of sugar if using dried yeast. Beat the eggs together with the sugar until light and creamy-coloured. Add the oil, butter, yeast and vanilla essence, then the semolina.

Sprinkle your hands well with orange-flower water, then form balls of the paste about the size of a walnut, using plenty of the fragrant orange-flower water.

Flatten each ball, then coat one side of each with icing sugar. Arrange on a greased baking sheet, sugared side up. Leave to prove for about 30 minutes then bake for 15-20 minutes at 180°C, 350°F/Gas 4.

Griouches (see p. 73)

Another Moroccan sweet delight, popular during Ramadan, these are simple to make and keep very well.

25 g (1 oz) fresh yeast or
$\frac{1}{2}$ as much dried yeast
3 egg yolks
125 g (4 oz) sugar
50 g (2 oz) sesame seeds,
$\frac{3}{4}$ of them ground or
pounded fine
80 ml (3 fl oz) wine vinegar
450 g (1 lb) strong white
flour
peanut oil
honey
orange-flower water
(optional)
saffron
melted butter (optional)

Activate the yeast in a little warm water, adding a pinch of sugar if using dried yeast. When it is frothy, mix in the egg yolks, sugar, sesame seeds and vinegar, adding, if desired, a few teaspoons of orange-flower water and a good pinch of saffron. Add the flour and use the peanut oil to make up into a rather firmer dough than that used for bread-making. Leave to rise, covered with a damp cloth, for about 2 hours. Roll out the dough to about 5 mm ($\frac{1}{4}$ in) thick. First cut the

dough into pieces about 20×12 cm (8×5 in). Leaving a 2-5 cm (1-in) border top and bottom, make 6 cuts in the dough to give 7 strips.

Thread the index finger of one hand through each alternate strand and lift the dough from the table.

With the other hand, take two opposite corners, then pinch together firmly. Now unthread your finger and put the dough down, disregarding the shape into which it

now falls. Follow the same procedure for each griouche —every one will be a different shape. Then leave them to rise for 30 minutes.

Heat a deep pan of oil and deep-fry the griouches, several at a time (or shallow-fry if preferred). Lift them straight from the oil with a slotted spatula, then drain

quickly. Whilst still hot, plunge them into a saucepan of clear honey which has been brought to the boil and then stood close to the source of heat to keep hot. When each is sated with honey, remove and drain on a wire rack.

Sprinkle the griouches with browned sesame seeds while they are still warm.

Chebbakia (see p. 73)

These are another honeyed Moorish treat. Make some loukoumades dough (see p. 72) that is soft enough to slither through a funnel. Leave to prove, then fill the funnel with dough, blocking the hole with a finger. Hold the funnel above a pan of very hot oil.

Then let the dough trickle into the fat, quickly tracing a

pattern: flowers are traditional, though not easy.

When brown on both sides (you may have to turn it), lift the shape out with a perforated spoon, quickly drain and plunge into very hot honey for 1 minute.

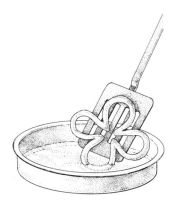

Rather than soaking through the pastry as with griouches, the honey will collect in little pockets in the hollow parts of the chebbakia; it explodes in bursts as you eat it.
India has its own version of chebbakia. The shape is a figure of eight and the honey is replaced by a syrup of sugar, water saffron and crushed cardamom.

Coconut coffee twist
15 g ($\frac{1}{2}$ oz) fresh yeast or $\frac{1}{2}$ as much dried yeast
275 ml ($\frac{1}{2}$ pint) mixed milk and water
450 g (1 lb) strong white flour
80 g (3 oz) desiccated coconut
25 g (1 oz) white sugar
15 g ($\frac{1}{2}$ oz) salt
a little honey or molasses

Mix the yeast and sugar with the liquid. Mix together the flour, coconut and salt. Add the yeast liquid when frothy and make rather a firm dough, adding more flour if necessary. Knead until light and elastic.
Leave to double in size in a warm place, covered.
Knock down and knead lightly on a floured board, then divide into three equal pieces. Roll into three long strips, plait, then form into a circle and put on a greased and floured baking sheet.
Leave to double in size in a cold place for 12 hours or so (it may go out of shape if it rises too quickly).
Bake at 220°C, 450°F/ Gas 8 for 40-45 minutes.
While still hot, brush with honey or molasses.
Coconut coffee twist can be decorated, when cold, with more coconut (toasted coconut is good) or toasted flaked almonds. Alterna- tively, coat with a lemon- or orange-flavoured icing.

Hawkshead cake
This English cake is a re- minder of the days when most heavy fruit cakes were leavened with yeast. Make it only for a special occasion: the amount of yeast it con- tains will prevent it keeping.
50 g (2 oz) fresh yeast
800 g (1 lb 12 oz) strong white flour
350 g (12 oz) butter or margarine
225 g (8 oz) soft brown sugar
pinch salt
125 g (4 oz) sultanas
450 g (1 lb) currants
50 g (2 oz) candied peel
about 450 ml ($\frac{3}{4}$ pint) warm, scalded milk

Rub the fresh yeast into the flour.
Rub the butter or mar- garine into the flour/yeast mixture, then mix in the sugar and salt. Mix in the fruit, which should be lightly floured, then add warm milk to make a soft dough.
Put into well-greased shallow tins and allow to rise in a warm place for about 40 minutes. Bake in a mod- erate oven, 180°C, 350°F/ Gas 4 for 30-40 minutes.
Variations This recipe, with its relatively large amount of yeast, is one of expediency and must be eaten quickly. You would achieve just as good a result by using rather less yeast and leaving it all to rise longer in a cool place.
A handful or two of wholemeal flour to replace some of the white flour is good in this cake. Soaking the fruit in rum or cream sherry for a few hours is also recommended.

Moreland Close crunchy cake

This is an English version of Austria's streusel. The topping can be used on any fruity, spicy mixture.

Cake:
- 225 g (8 oz) strong white flour
- 50 g (2 oz) fine semolina
- 50 g (2 oz) white sugar
- 25 g (1 oz) fresh yeast
- 80 g (3 oz) butter or margarine
- 2 eggs
- 80 ml (3 fl oz) lukewarm milk, previously scalded
- 50 g (2 oz) currants
- grated rind of 1 sweet orange
- jam

Topping:
- 50 g (2 oz) strong white flour
- 50 g (2 oz) white sugar
- 50 g (2 oz) butter or margarine
- 15 g (½ oz) cinnamon

Mix the flour, semolina and sugar together, then rub in first the yeast, then the butter or margarine. Beat the eggs together, add the milk, then beat this into the flour with a wooden spoon to make a soft dough. Lightly mix in the currants and orange rind.

Turn the mixture into a buttered shallow baking tin and spread evenly, using wetted fingers. Spread the jam thinly over the top, warming it first if necessary.

Now rub together the topping ingredients and sprinkle evenly on top.

Leave to prove for about 30 minutes or until doubled in size. Bake in a hottish

oven (220°C, 425°F/Gas 7) for 30-40 minutes.

Even though this is a cake, it is delicious hot, spread with butter, and can be toasted, too.

Variations Replace the jam with honey or even with a layer of fresh soft fruits, such as blackcurrants. Substitute some wholemeal, rye or buckwheat flour, or add wheat grains or oatmeal, to give the cake an individual flavour. Try serving with cream.

Bath buns

- 25 g (1 oz) fresh yeast or ½ as much dried yeast
- 2 eggs
- 80 ml (3 fl oz) warm milk
- 150 g (5 oz) melted butter
- 450 g (1 lb) strong or soft white flour
- 125 g (4 oz) sugar (or less)
- pinch salt
- 1 egg, beaten
- a little milk
- crushed lump sugar
- sultanas (optional)
- mixed peel (optional)
- grated lemon peel (optional)

Activate the yeast in a little water, adding a pinch of sugar if using dried yeast. Whisk the eggs, warm milk and butter together. Mix into the sifted flour, sugar and salt. Add the yeast. Knead well. Leave to double in size.

Divide into twelve, leave to prove until doubled in size on a greased baking tray. Brush with beaten egg mixed with a little milk and crushed lump sugar. Bake at 190°C, 375°F/Gas 5 for 15-20 minutes.

Variations The amount of sultanas, peel or rind used can be varied: a total of about 250 g (7-8 oz) is enough fruit, but the peel of one lemon would suffice, finely grated. Chopped mixed peel can be used on its own. Never use currants.

Chelsea buns (see p. 72)
Make the same dough as for Bath buns, using half the amount of sugar and flavouring it with the grated peel (zest) of a small lemon and 5 g (1 teaspoon) mixed spice.

While it is rising, prepare the filling from:

- 80 g (3 oz) melted butter
- 80 g (3 oz) currants
- 80 g (3 oz) brown sugar

When the dough has risen once, knead it lightly and roll out to a rectangle three times longer than it is wide (it may be easier to divide the dough and make two rectangles). Brush with melted butter, mix the currants and brown sugar and spread evenly.

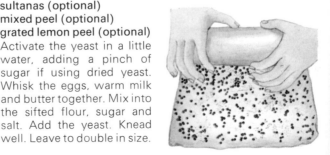

(**Optional stage** Fold and roll the dough several times, as in making puff pastry or croissants. This method gives lighter, airy buns and adds the delight of a little mystery, as the currants cannot be seen.)

Now roll up the dough firmly like a Swiss roll, cut into slices and lay these on a greased baking sheet so that they just touch when they have risen and doubled in size, which should take about 30-45 minutes.

When the buns are ready they should be baked at 220°C, 425°F/Gas 7 for 15-20 minutes, by which time they should finally have joined together in the traditional cube-like shapes.

Brush with a glaze made by boiling equal quantities of milk and sugar until thickened. (Warmed honey is just as effective.) Sprinkle with castor sugar.

Sally Lunn

A light sweet bread of this name originated in the West of England. There are countless versions, including French ones, and just as many stories about the origin of the name. Either there really was someone called Sally Lunn who hawked these delicacies through the streets of Bath, or the name is a corruption of 'sol et lune', for these breads are thought to look like the sun and moon if made properly—a rich, shining, golden top and a pale, delicate base.

The first, traditional, method is started one morning and finished the next.

(1) Traditional Sally Lunn

15 g (½ oz) fresh yeast
125 g (4 oz) strong white flour
a little warm, scalded milk
350 g (12 oz) strong white flour
15 g (½ oz) salt
15 g (½ oz) sugar
5 g (1 teaspoon) mixed spice
225 ml (8 fl oz) milk direct from the cow, or warm double cream

Early in the morning, crumble the yeast into a small bowl, add the first quantity of flour and work to a cream with a little warm milk, previously scalded. Cover and leave in a warm (not hot) place.

In another bowl, mix the second amount of flour with the salt, sugar and spices; cover.

In the evening, make a dough with the spiced flour and the fresh milk or cream. Work the dough into a flat shape, then spread with the yeast mixture. Knead lightly together, cover and leave to rise overnight in a warm place.

Next morning, knead once more, very lightly, shape into one large or several smaller round buns and put into appropriate tins. Cover and leave until well risen. Brush the top with beaten egg yolk only. Bake until golden brown only—about 15 minutes at 180°C, 350°F/Gas 4, depending on the sizes of the tins used. Remove from tins, scatter with crushed cube sugar and cool on a rack.

Split, then fill with cream beaten with the egg white left over from the glaze.

Variations Many old recipes also include eggs, giving something more like brioche. Add up to three eggs and reduce the amount of milk or cream used.

(2) Modern Sally Lunn

Starting with 450 g (1 lb) strong white flour, make a dough in the usual way with the same proportions as the previous recipe. Allow the dough to rise once, then shape, prove and bake. Eggs may be incorporated.

Lardy cake

Lardy cakes are an incredibly tempting way, especially on a cold day, to ensure over-indulgence in sugar and cholesterol!

680 g (1½ lb) white bread
   dough, risen once
or
a dough made of
   450 g (1 lb) flour and
   15 g (½ oz) fresh yeast, or
   ½ as much dried yeast
   5 g (1 teaspoon) salt
   water
plus
125 g (4 oz) lard
125 g (4 oz) brown or
   white sugar
125 g (4 oz) sultanas, or
   mixed fruit

Roll the dough into a rectangle, spread one-third of the lard, sugar and fruit over two-thirds of the dough and fold into three (see croissant instructions on p. 62). Roll out and repeat twice. Leave the lardy cake to rest and rise for 30 minutes, then roll out once more. Now roll it up like a Swiss roll. Leave to double in size, covered with a towel, either in a bread tin or, cut in two, cut-side down, in 12·5-cm (5-in) round tins. Score deeply

where you will eventually wish to separate into cakes.

Bake at 205°C, 400°F/ Gas 6 for about ¾ hour.

If the cooked cake is swimming in lard, leave it in the tins for a few minutes while the lard is absorbed. Otherwise turn it out. The cake will break where it has been scored, and should never be divided with a knife.

Poppy-seed loaf (see p.73)

This great mid-European favourite is very much at home in the United States and Canada too.

10 g (¼ oz) fresh yeast or ½
   as much dried yeast
85 ml (3 fl oz) lukewarm
   milk, previously scalded
50 g (2 oz) butter
100 g (4 oz) sugar
5 ml (1 teaspoon) salt
225 g (8 oz) strong white
   flour
3 egg yolks, beaten
rind of one lemon, grated
50 g (2 oz) unsalted butter
25 ml (1 fl oz) clear honey
a little double cream
175 g (6 oz) roasted poppy
   seeds
50 g (2 oz) grated orange
   rind or chopped,
   crystallized orange peel
100 g (4 oz) crushed or
   chopped almonds
2 egg whites

Activate the yeast with some of the warm milk, adding a pinch of sugar if using dried yeast. Melt the 50 g (2 oz) butter in the remaining milk. Dissolve the sugar and salt in this and keep warm. Make a well in the middle of the warmed flour, pour in the yeast and milk mixtures,

plus the beaten egg yolks and lemon rind. Gradually mix the flour into the liquid, using your hands.

Knead the mixture until it is elastic and satin-like. Leave the dough to double in size.

If you have not been able to buy the poppy seeds ready-roasted, simply put them into a medium-hot oven and keep turning them over until they are ready.

Cream together the butter and honey and add just a trickle of thick cream. Mix in the poppy seeds, orange and almonds.

Beat one egg white until stiff, then fold this into the mix. Punch down and knead the dough, then roll it out to a rectangle about 35 × 20 cm (14 × 8 in) which should be about 1 cm (just under ½ in) thick.

Spread the seed and nut mixture evenly on the dough, allowing a border all round. Moisten this border with milk. Roll up the dough (from one of the narrow sides). Seal the ends and the join with a little pressure. Put the roll, seam down, on a baking sheet. Tuck the ends under if they are a little untidy, but avoid doing so if possible.

Cover with a damp cloth and leave until doubled in size again—about 45 minutes in a reasonably warm, but not hot, place.

Brush with the other egg white, lightly beaten. Bake for 40 minutes at 180°C, 350°F/Gas 4. The loaf should be a very deep golden brown. Glaze again, if need be, just before you take it out. The loaf should be cooled completely before being served.

Variations Ground hazelnuts and chopped almonds

or any other mixture of chopped and ground nuts are delicious with the poppy seeds, or instead of them. Lemon can be used in the mixture.

Polish babke or baba
This flourless, saffron-flavoured yeast sponge is a triumph if you can do it!
25 g (1 oz) fresh yeast or
½ as much dried yeast
150 ml (5 fl oz) lukewarm
milk previously scalded
8 egg yolks
100 g (4 oz) castor sugar
a few drops vanilla essence
pinch ground saffron

5 g (½ teaspoon) salt
100 g (4 oz) melted butter
Activate the yeast in some of the warm milk, adding a pinch of sugar if using dried yeast. Beat the egg yolks and sugar over hot water until thick and white. Add all the other ingredients, except the butter, to the eggs. Beat well. Pour in the butter and beat well again. Place the mixture in a greased

tin (a tall, fluted tin with a central spout is best); it should fill the tin by no more than one-third. Cover and leave to double in size in a warm place. Bake in a hot oven for 1 hour.

Omit the saffron if wished.

Gugelhopf
Rich, Austrian and found in hundreds of versions, *Gugelhopf* is the word for almost any yeast cake cooked in a fluted, centre-tube mould.
25 g (1 oz) fresh yeast or
½ as much dried yeast
200 ml (7 fl oz) warm milk
125 g (4 oz) butter
5 egg yolks
350 g (12 oz) strong white
flour
125 g (4 oz) sugar

pinch salt
100 g (4 oz) stoned raisins
grated rind of 1 orange
a little cornflour
50 g (2 oz) blanched
almonds
Activate the yeast in the milk, adding a pinch of sugar if using dried yeast.

Soften the butter slightly, beat the egg yolks in slowly, alternating with the flour.

Then add the sugar and salt, beat in well and add the raisins and grated orange rind. Gently fold in the yeast mixture.

Quickly butter a 25-cm (10-in)-deep fluted, centre-tube mould. Dust with cornflour, then scatter with the chopped almonds and put the mixture in the tin.

Stand in a warm place to rise, covered with a large bowl. When the mixture has doubled in size, bake at 180°C, 350°F/Gas 4 for 45-60 minutes until firm.

Turn the cake out as soon as it comes from the oven and cool on a wire rack.

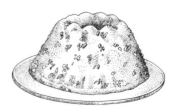

Berliner kranzküchen

(p. 73)

This golden 'garland' cake is a yeasted strudel fragrant with rose-water icing.

40 g (1½ oz) fresh yeast or ½ as much dried yeast
50 ml (2 fl oz) milk or water
175 g (6 oz) butter
450 g (1 lb) strong white flour
5 egg yolks
50 g (2 oz) castor sugar
25 g (1 oz) butter, melted
175 g (6 oz) ground almonds
350 g (12 oz) currants
175 g (6 oz) castor sugar
icing sugar/rose water

Activate the yeast in the warm milk or water, adding a pinch of sugar if using dried yeast. Rub the butter into the flour until it looks like fine breadcrumbs. Beat the egg yolks with the sugar until smooth. Add the yeast mixture and stir until sugar is fully dissolved. Work into the flour.

Knead very well until very smooth and elastic.

Leave to prove for about 1 hour. For rolling out, you need a large, flat surface, at least 2 x 2 m (6 x 6 ft). Failing this, divide the

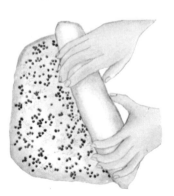

dough into an even number of smaller amounts.

Roll out the dough or portion of dough into a long rectangle, as thin as possible (you should be able to see through it). Brush with melted butter, scatter with chopped or ground nuts, currants and sugar.

Roll up from one of the long sides to make a thin sausage. The dough can be very difficult to manage at this stage, so you may need to ask someone to help you. If you have made just one sausage, cut it in half, otherwise repeat for the remaining dough.

Now twist the two strands round each other to form a circle or wreath. Leave to rise on a baking tray, covered. Glaze with egg yolk and bake at 180°C, 350°F/Gas 4 for 40 minutes.

When the cake is cold, cover with a white icing made with rose water.

Creole rice cakes

These yeasted rice cakes are served hot for breakfast in New Orleans.

125 g (4 oz) rice
750 ml (24 fl oz) water
25 g (1 oz) fresh yeast
3 eggs
25-50 g (1-2 oz) strong white flour
50-75 g (2-3 oz) sugar, according to taste
oil or lard for deep-frying

Slowly cook the rice in the water until mushy, without straining off the water. When cold, dissolve the yeast in a little warm water, add to the rice mush, cover and leave overnight.

In the morning, beat up the eggs very well and add to the rice with the flour and sugar to make a thick batter. Leave to rise for about 20-30 minutes, then deep-fry one large spoonful at a time. Drain, keep hot, then serve sprinkled with a little more sugar.

Variations These are many, created by different types of rice, flour and sugar.

Sand- wiches

A little imagination can go a long way where sandwiches are concerned. The ideas here should give you plenty of scope for the next occasion on which you entertain. The Danes, with their genius for edible ingenuity, have always been paramount where sandwiches are concerned. Some of their open sandwiches are substantial enough for a family lunch or snack.

Silhouette sandwiches

A simple, intriguing idea for decorative open-face sandwiches—but you do˙need sharp pastry or canapé cutters.

For 8 sandwiches

8 slices fresh bread
butter or margarine
pickle or chutney spread
6-8 slices pre-packed ham
4 slices pre-packed cheese

Cut the crusts from the bread and butter each slice right to the edges. Smear on a little pickle or chutney. Lay ham on each of the slices.

Now cut a shape out of a slice of cheese with a shaped cutter. Put the slice with the hole in it on top of one slice of ham; put the cut-out shape on next. Repeat with a different cutter. To finish, trim any unsightly edges and add tomato or parsley for colour or decoration.

Variations If you want to make a lot of these sandwiches there are many ways of ringing the changes. Use

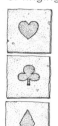

8 slices of cheese and 4 of ham and cut the shapes from the meat. Or try combinations of meat—ham and tongue over a spicy tomato chutney makes a lovely sandwich. Note that the meat should be approximately the size and shape of the bread and able to be cut with your cutters.

Pinwheel sandwiches

A great favourite whenever they appear, pinwheels are so simple to make that even children can do them. In fact, if you are busy, children are usually glad to help out by making them. The classic pinwheel is smoked salmon in brown bread. But even jam on white bread looks good—on Guy Fawkes' Night you could call them catherine wheels !

For 4-6 small pinwheels

2 slices very fresh bread
butter or margarine
sandwich filling

Cut the crusts off the slices and butter right to the edges.

Choose a filling that contrasts with the bread, spread or arrange right to the edges then roll one slice tightly, though not so tightly that the filling comes out. Butt the end of the second slice against the end of the rolled slice and continue rolling. Secure the whole with cock-

tail sticks or toothpicks. Now continue with other breads and other fillings.

Leave the rolls for at least an hour in a cool place, covered with a damp cloth. Then cut them into slices, as you would a Swiss roll. You can remove the sticks or leave them in and press them into a half grapefruit so they look like lollipops.

Variations When you are expert at rolling, roll the sandwiches round something. For instance, spread a lemon- or dill-flavoured cream cheese on brown bread and roll round an asparagus spear.

Spread mashed sardines and roll the first slice round chopped olives. Rolling in this way produces bigger sandwiches and a colourful centre.

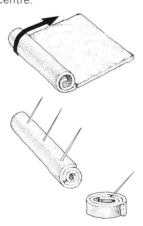

Toasted sandwiches

There are two distinct schools of thought regarding these: according to one, the bread is toasted first, before making the sandwiches; according to the other, the sandwiches are made and then toasted. The latter is far better, but requires a grill as opposed to a toaster.

The difference stems from the fact that when a sandwich is made of toast, the filling will not be hot unless it is heated separately, which is wasteful of energy and cuts down the range of fillings you can use, whereas when a toasted sandwich is cooked slowly under a grill, the filling will heat through well.

For example, if a toasted sandwich containing cheese is cooked in a grill, the cheese melts, smells wonderful and makes an altogether more satisfying sandwich, especially if drained crushed pineapple, a slice of ham or slices of tomato have been added to the cheese.

Almost any sandwich filling is suitable for toasted sandwiches. But there is a cardinal rule. Always butter the top of the sandwich, on the outside, while it is still hot, whichever way you have made your toasted sandwich. Otherwise the two slices of toast will almost always seem too dry and woolly in the mouth.

Tea sandwiches

Elegant sandwiches were always essential components of the elegant teas of yesterday. Cucumber and cress were *de rigueur*.

Today, it creates a sensation to present a patterned plateful of thin sandwiches.

The main requirements are an exceptionally sharp knife, time and imagination.

If you have trouble cutting bread thinly, try taking the crusts off *first*.

The illustrations below show the pretty effects you can make on a plate by using two types of bread.

Perfect party loaf

Depending on your choice of sweet or savoury fillings, this impressive-looking creation is suitable for either children or adults.

1 oblong, unsliced loaf of bread, 1 day old, 15 cm (6 in) long
175 g (6 oz) cream cheese
30 ml (6 teaspoons) milk
butter
up to 3 different fillings
chopped parsley, nuts

First cut off all 6 crusts and put the loaf on its side. Slice it lengthwise: the first slice cut will be the equivalent of a thin layer off the bottom of the loaf. Keep going, keeping the slices as even as possible. Try to get at least 9, though 12 is preferable, slices out of the loaf.

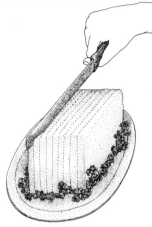

Put the bottom (first) slice on to the plate on which you intend to serve the loaf. Butter this slice, then butter every other slice except the top (last) slice on both sides (butter the last slice only on *one* side).

To make, spread a filling on the bottom slice of bread, then add a slice buttered on both sides, spread another filling, add another slice and so on. Then add the top slice, buttered side down.

Put the cream cheese into a bowl, mash it and add the milk to get a good spreading consistency.

Spread the cheese over the loaf top and sides. You can make an attractive pattern simply by dragging a fork over the cheese. Leave in a cool place for at least 1 hour but no longer than 4 hours.

Before serving, sprinkle with a mixture of chopped parsley and nuts, for a savoury loaf, or, for a sweet loaf, just nuts. If the bottom of the loaf looks a little ragged, arrange sprigs of parsley or other decoration around it.

Serve by slicing thinly, perhaps using a spatula or egg slice to help serve the slices.

Variations It is best to contrast textures and colours. Children seem to like a variety of spreads and pastes: mashed bananas are popular; so is peanut butter with a fruity jam and a smooth jelly. Always try to use a filling that is spreadable, because sliced meats can be difficult to cut through when serving.

Among the ingredients to use for more special occasions are savoury spreads based on cheese; chopped olives and chicken; fish pâtés; smoked salmon; flaked smoked trout; thin cucumber slices; potted meats; and drained crushed pineapple teamed with cheese.

For added interest you could always flavour the cheese covering, too. Try sweet paprika and chopped gherkins; tomato paste, crushed garlic and oreganum; chives; celery salt, crumbled crispy bacon, or curry powder with a little grated orange peel. Those with the time and talent can really go to town decorating the finished loaf, too.

Cut each slice in half if they look too big.

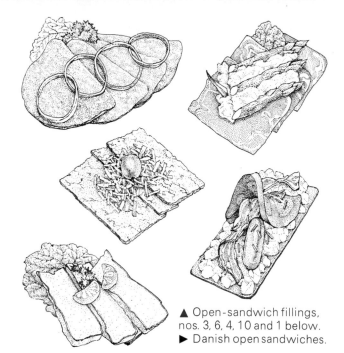

▲ Open-sandwich fillings, nos. 3, 6, 4, 10 and 1 below.
▶ Danish open sandwiches.

Danish open sandwiches

There are no rules for these sandwiches. The bread can be rye, black, stone-ground or white, or some of each; you can use rye crisps or pumpernickel slices, toast, or pre-packed sliced bread. The practicalities of eating the sandwiches should never be allowed to inhibit creativity: the Danes *expect* to have to eat open sandwiches with a knife and fork.

The base is most important. Butter or margarine is good but mayonnaise gives a richer and more interesting effect. Lettuce leaves, cottage or cream cheese on butter or mayonnaise are useful, as you can rest other items against them.

The following combinations can be decorated with small pieces of lettuce,

strips of tomato, sprigs of parsley, twists of lemon, radish roses or gherkins.

(1) Brie, mandarin orange, lettuce, parsley.
(2) Gammon slice, scrambled egg, chives, tomato and cucumber.
(3) Salami, onion rings, lettuce and parsley.
(4) Blue cheese, grated carrot and black grapes.
(5) Sliced herring fillet, onion rings, sour cream.
(6) Thin ham, asparagus in lemony mayonnaise, lettuce, parsley.
(7) Ham, spiced peach, fresh pineapple, made mustard.
(8) Sliced brawn, potato salad, cress, radish.
(9) Sliced tongue, ham strips in garlic mayonnaise, raw mushrooms.
(10) Cocktail sausage, bacon, lettuce, potato salad.

Bread in your diet

White bread is regarded as an excellent source of energy, protein and the B vitamins, plus minerals and trace elements. The bran, wheatgerm and wheatgerm oil content of wholemeal bread provides, in addition, Vitamin E. As calcium is added to all flours in the UK, bread is also, for the British, a significant source of calcium.

So-called brown bread is usually made with white flour coloured with caramel. However, it usually contains some bran or malted grains as well, and thiamin and nicotinic acid have been replaced in the flour to give it the same vitamin content as an 80% extraction flour. This puts its dietary value somewhere between that of white and wholemeal breads.

Bread contains no Vitamins A, D, B_{12} or C and the expected bonus of extra vitamins and minerals in wholemeal bread can be a forlorn hope.

Life supporter

No evidence exists to support the common assumption that wholemeal bread is good for you while white bread is damaging to your health. Wholemeal bread does contain bran, however, and should offer both Vitamin E and a higher proportion of minerals and trace elements than white. In practice, according to some dieticians, wholemeal bread could actually be detrimental to health. It seems we are likely to spread it more thickly with butter, jam and other good-tasting comestibles than we might mundane white bread; arguments exist to show that such excesses are far worse for us than the suspected chemical shortcomings of white bread! Research in the USA shows that as long as the rest of the diet has a minimal proportion of high-quality protein, a white bread diet successfully supports life and encourages excellent growth in 5- to 15-year-olds.

During the Second World War, it was thought that high-extraction flour (the only type then milled) caused rickets in children. This theory is not far-fetched. Wholemeal flour contains a substance called phytic acid, which is present in the whole grain. In the bowels, this phytic acid locks itself on to valuable calcium, iron and magnesium, preventing the body from absorbing and using them. The British government decreed that chalk, in the form of highly refined calcium carbonate, should be added to all flours other than wholemeal at a rate three times higher than daily requirements. It is still added today, for although the war-time rickets scare has passed, chalk is thought to help prevent some heart diseases.

Additives to flour

The many additives to white flour used throughout the world fall into two categories. Some substances are added for dietary reasons, to redress an imbalance produced in the processing of the flour, some to improve the performance and commercial appeal of the flour.

Dietary additives are usually thiamin (Vitamin B_1), nicotinic acid, riboflavin and iron in certain proportions. There is no international agreement about levels of additives; the level of vitamins added to flour in the UK is far lower than that used in the USA, and Scandinavia insists on twice the amount of riboflavin used in the latter.

Slimming breads

Often called starch-reduced breads, these are made with flour to which extra gluten has been added. Today there is a tendency to call them 'high-protein' breads, for the sake of accuracy. The high proportion of gluten they contain produces a bulkier, more aerated loaf than regular flour. If you eat high-protein breads, slice for slice you will be eating more air and less bread; by eating fewer slices of ordinary bread, you would cut down your starch intake just as effectively. Ounce for ounce, high-protein breads have calorie values equivalent to those of other breads.

Diet breads

Salt-free and gluten-free breads do provide a useful element in certain—though not in slimming—special diets. Salt-free bread is most helpful in some heart conditions but is not terribly palatable and is not easy to buy.

Gluten-free flour, usually available only on prescription, is most important in the diets of coeliac sufferers. Coeliac disease is caused by malabsorption, and sufferers cannot digest the gliadin in gluten. The difficulties of baking with this flour can be helped to some extent by the addition of gluten-free protein such as milk.

Leavening wholemeal bread

Wholemeal breads should always be made with yeast rather than baking soda. Yeast-risen wholemeal bread breaks down some of the potentially troublesome phytic acid, which the quick-mixed soda bread cannot do. Soda also destroys Vitamin E, one of the principal reasons for choosing wholemeal flour.

Dough additives

Additives permitted in bread dough (United Kingdom)

Additive (example)	Function	Technical name
sorbic acid	prevention of mould growth	preservative
caramel	colouring white dough to make 'brown' bread	colouring
lecithin	even blending of ingredients	emulsifier
malt, soya, amylases	balancing enzyme content of flour to get consistency	enzymes
ammonium chloride calcium sulphate	promotion of vigorous yeast growth	yeast stimulants
various chemicals contained in fats used in bread-making	prevention of rankness in fats	anti-oxidants
starch	carrying agent for other additives	excipients

Note All these additives may be found in wholemeal bread. No bleach or improvers are permitted in wholemeal flour or bread, neither may chalk, gluten, wheatgerm, cereal or nutrients be added. Sugar may be added to all bread doughs.

Guide to rising times

21°C, 70°F and over	**1½-2 hours**
18°C, 64°F (room temperature)	**2-3 hours+**
10°C, 50°F (e.g. larder)	**up to 12 hours**
refrigerator	**up to 24 hours**

Wholemeal flours do not benefit from extended rising, but all other flours do. This table is a rough guide to how long a dough made with 450-675 g (1-1½ lb) white or 85% flour and up to 15 g (½ oz) fresh yeast will take to rise for the first time. (Second risings are usually faster.) Doughs with a high proportion of yeast, such as brioche or croissant mixes, will rise much faster. If you intend to give your dough a long rising, use water that is only just lukewarm. Too much variation of temperature of the dough may have an adverse effect. Always allow refrigerated dough to reach room temperature before continuing with your recipe.

Leavening equivalents
Readers who wish to try out recipes from cookbooks printed before the advent of compressed (fresh) yeast are advised to work backwards from the amount of flour required. For bread doughs, 25 g (1 oz) fresh yeast is more than enough for 1·5 kg (3·31 lb). You can double the amount for sweet brioche-type doughs and sweet buns and cakes. The old yeasts and barms, measured by the pint or cup, contained liquid, so you may have to add extra water, milk or egg if you are adapting an old recipe and using compressed yeast instead of the old types.

Flour additives

Additives permitted in all flours, except wholemeal, in the United Kingdom

Additive	Function	Comments
ammonium persulphate	strengthens gluten	minimal usage, mainly Scotland and N. England
ascorbic acid (Vitamin C)	strengthens gluten	widely used in the new 'fast-dough' techniques
azodicarbonamide	strengthens gluten	newly permitted; mainly in new techniques
benzoyl peroxide	bleach	widely used, destroys Vitamin E
chlorine	bleach; strengthens gluten	used only in commercial cake flour
chlorine dioxide	bleach; strengthens gluten	widely used, often combined with benzoyl dioxide; destroys Vitamin E
L cysteine hydrochloride	weakens gluten	combined with ascorbic acid in new techniques
potassium bromate	strengthens gluten	widely used with the two main bleaches
sulphur dioxide	weakens gluten; preservative	used only in biscuit-making

Note It should be remembered that these additives are in no way connected with the synthetic vitamins and minerals which are also found in white flours.

Flour composition

Approximate composition of flour used in UK bread-making (at 15% moisture content)

	Wholemeal	Brown	White	Wholemeal (from all-British wheat)
assume extraction rate %	100	85-90	72	100
protein %	12·0	11·8	11·3	8·9
fat %	2·4	1·6	1·0	2·2
carbohydrate %	64·3	68·5	71·5	67·0
crude fibre %	2·0	1·09	0·12	1·8
dietary fibre %	11·2	7·87	3·15	11·2
ash %	1·5	1·37*	0·66*	1·5
total Ca mg/100 g	30	150†	140*	35
Fe mg/100 g	3·5	3·6	2·2‡	3·0
thiamin	0·40	0·42	0·31‡	0·29
nicotinic acid mg/100 g	5·5	4·2	2·0‡	4·8
riboflavin mg	0·12	0·06	0·03	0·12
Na mg/100 g	3·3	4·0	3·0	3·4
K mg/100 g	329	280	130	361
Mg mg/100 g	129	110	36	106
Cu mg/100 g	0·625	0·35	0·22	0·65
P mg/100 g	345	270	130	340
Cl mg/100 g	37	45	62	35
Mn mg/100 g	3·4	2·5	0·8	2·8

Ca = Calcium
Fe = Iron
Na = Sodium
K = Potassium
Mg = Magnesium
Cu = Copper
P = Phosphorus
Cl = Chlorine
Mn = Manganese

The addition of chalk at the rate of 235-390 mg/100 g is compulsory to all flours except wholemeal.
*Including 0·24 per cent derived from added chalk.
†Including 125 mg/100 g derived from added chalk*
‡Part of the iron, thiamin and nicotinic acid is derived from added nutrients

What went wrong?

If your bread does not turn out quite right, there may be a number of reasons rather than just one. Here is a guide to the most common faults in finished loaves, which should help you to detect where you went wrong.

The flying top
Uneven rising in the oven leads to a crust that has lifted in a long split, or bread which has an unsightly bulge.

The usual reason for this is unsuccessful rising before baking, and in most cases it is caused by too short a rising time. If you are never certain exactly when your dough has doubled in bulk, mark the tin accordingly when you put in the dough. Then let it take its time to reach that mark.

Close, heavy texture
This, too, is often caused by under-proving the uncooked dough. In white bread it may also mean insufficient kneading. It is also possible that the yeast has been killed prematurely because the dough was left to rise in too hot a place. Too much salt will have the same effect. If the loaf is simply rather drier than you expected, then you may have overcooked it.

Uneven texture with holes
Some people rather like holes in their bread, usually because they take up a lot of butter! If you want an even-textured loaf, with no large holes, take special care over knocking back, punching down and

re-kneading. The purpose of this is to distribute the yeast through the dough after the first rising.

The other main cause of bad texture, or streaks and stripes, is over-proving. Dough is proved to the right point when a light impression made with the forefinger soon disappears, as the dough springs back into its original shape.

Remember always to grease lightly and cover dough while it is rising, otherwise the crust that forms will make streaks in the bread. Streaks can also be caused by adding in flour during kneading without mixing it in thoroughly.

Coarse, dull-looking bread
This is usually the result of over-proving, or of over-activity of yeast caused by insufficient salt. If it is white bread that has disappointed, it may not have been kneaded enough: it is essential to keep going until you feel the texture change and become satiny.

Sour or yeasty flavour
This characteristic is typical of the sad-looking loaf last described. It is invariably caused by using too much yeast, and often by over-proving as well. Users of dried yeast who have been slack with measuring are sure to have come across such bread. Never be tempted to put in an extra grain or two of dried yeast. The rule is: if in doubt, take some out!

Fast staling
This will almost certainly be caused by using too much yeast. Too fast a rise will make the finished bread stale quickly, too.

Warm storage and low or no fat can also cause fast staling.

Cold storage

Careful use of a refrigerator or home freezer, or both, will guarantee you a constant supply of yeast or baked goods. Neither appliance will save you much time, but you will be able to bake just when it suits you, weekly, fortnightly or even less often if you have the storage capacity.

Refrigerating yeast
If it is easy for you to buy yeast, then buy exactly the quantity you want, when you want it. If you have to store it, use the coldest part of the refrigerator. Provided the yeast was in good condition and you have bought a good-sized piece, it should last a full two weeks.

Some air circulation helps storage of yeast, so either wrap it loosely in greaseproof paper or store it in a fairly close-fitting container with a little ventilation. Keep it away from strong odours. Melon, slices of which are very often put into refrigerators unwrapped, is a particularly bad offender. There are few things that invade other foods quite so vigorously.

Refrigerating dough
If your bread making is interrupted for some hours, or overnight, and you have no room cold enough in which to inhibit the rising of the dough, put it in the refrigerator. It must be well wrapped, and should ideally be given a light coating of oil to stop the formation of a skin.

When you are ready to start again, let the dough get back to

▶ The kitchen of Wales' St Fagan's castle is typically medieval. The huge box with the open grid base suspended from the ceiling was used to store bread, allowing the free circulation of air which prevents mould growth. With reliable storage baking needed to be done only once or twice a week.

room temperature first, kneading extra well to ensure an even spread of temperature in the dough.

As yeasted dough works in refrigerator temperatures, never leave it more than 24 hours without punching it down and kneading.

Provided the salt content of the dough is relatively high you can keep dough in the refrigerator for a couple of days or more as long as you knead it whenever it has doubled in bulk.

Refrigerating bread
Although very popular, the storage of bread in the refrigerator is only an advantage over very short periods. Refrigerators inhibit the growth of mould but withdraw moisture; any apparent moistness detected in the mouth is more probably condensation!

Deep-freezing yeast
Those who find it difficult to obtain compressed yeast but own a freezer may safely splash out on yeast when they have the opportunity. Yeast freezes very well, and should produce excellent results for up to three months, possibly longer.

Pack the yeast in suitable sizes—say 25-g (1-oz) batches —and seal and label it carefully. Allow frozen yeast to thaw slowly, then dissolve it in lukewarm liquid as usual.

Deep-frozen dough
Dough made up with fresh yeast will freeze successfully, and will obviously take up less space than baked loaves in the freezer. As it is more economic to bake in batches rather than loaf by loaf, it is perhaps better to freeze cooked loaves rather than uncooked dough.

However, if your freezing capacity is limited, freeze dough in small containers of 6-12 made-up rolls. These will thaw and be ready for working and cooking far faster than a loaf; you could even add extra yeast to the mixture to ensure extra-fast rising, but this would mean losing the flavour advantage given by slow maturing and rising.

Whatever your decision, the dough must thaw, be kneaded, rise, be shaped, rise again, then be baked. No time is saved overall, but it can be saved at the point when time is shortest.

Deep-freezing bread
This is the perfect way to maintain the moisture content of bread, provided you freeze the loaf as soon as it is cool. Each loaf must be well sealed, and any type can be used, although crusty French loaves tend to crack and *must* be refreshed in the oven.

The dimensions of most domestic freezers dictate that tin loaves are most suitable for storing. They stack more easily, with almost no wasted space. Bread can be thawed either slowly at room temperature, or finished in the oven, or thawed entirely in the oven.

At room temperature a fairly large loaf will take anything up to four hours to thaw completely. Condensation will form inside the freezer bag and settle on the bread, which will affect the crust. The softened crust will shorten the life of the bread. To obtain a better crust, open the bag and take the bread out as soon as you can. Ten minutes in a moderate oven will finish the job and ensure that you avoid serving a loaf with an icy core.

When you need bread immediately and have no time to start unfreezing it at room temperature, transfer the bread directly from the freezer to the oven, unwrapped. Half an hour at a moderate temperature is usually enough, but use a metal skewer to check for a heart of iced or icy crumb.

If you wish, take this opportunity to glaze or re-glaze your loaf by brushing it over quickly with some milk or cream.

Suppliers

The following companies supply the more unusual flours and grains and many will also advise on related problems if you write to them.

W. Jordan and Son Ltd,
Holme Mills,
Biggleswade,
Bedfordshire
Biggleswade 312001
As well as making a range of unbleached flours in their water-driven roller mills, Jordan's sell a range of excellent bread tins and a recipe book. Their flour packs often carry good recipes and offers. Jordan's will also help with individual queries.

Allinson Ltd,
Queen's Mills,
Aire Street,
Castleford,
Yorkshire
Castleford 556277
Allinson's market a very wide range of specialist flours, including stone-ground wholemeal.

Ceres Grain Shop,
269 Portobello Road,
London W11
01-229 5571
Ceres, in Portobello Market, sell an astonishing range of flours and grains. Often they are packed on the premises and are therefore much cheaper than they would be elsewhere. Enthusiastic staff will give advice if they can. If you want to buy a hand mill so that you can grind your own grain, try phoning Ceres, who often have hand mills for sale.

Harmony Foods,
1 Earl Cottages,
London SE1
01-237 8396
Harmony is a well-known distributor of pure foods. Their wholemeal grains, millet and brown rice are recommended. Send a stamped addressed envelope for a free recipe brochure.

Prewett's Mill,
Worthing Road,
Horsham,
Sussex
Horsham 3208
Prewett's are rather more specialized millers than most. They market a complete range of cereals and flours, which are usually available in health or other special food shops rather than in supermarkets. The products are excellent, and Prewett's will also give advice on health food recipes if you write to them.

Equipment for bread-making is widely available. However, the following stores are specialists in kitchen equipment and should be able to help in case of difficulty. They can also supply the more unusual tins and moulds mentioned in this book.

Elizabeth David Ltd,
46 Bourne Street,
London SW1
01-730 3123

Divertimenti,
68-72 Marylebone Lane,
London W1
01-935 0689

David Mellor,
4 Sloane Square,
London SW1W 8EE
01-730 4259

Book list

Many short, inexpensive books or booklets are produced in the UK for local distribution and are well worth looking out for in wholefood or health-food shops. Always glance through these books before buying, however, for most of them contain simply minor variations on the same basic recipes.

Old recipe books and foreign books are the best field for research into unusual or traditional yeast cookery from other countries. Some embassies will give advice and even supply recipes in response to specific requests.

Amongst the bigger, more expensive books that are available you should have no trouble finding those on the following list, which are available through any bookshop.

English Bread and Yeast Cookery, Elizabeth David, Allen Lane, 1977, £6·50. A big, 591-page treatise that includes pizza, French bread and other foreign basics in spite of its title. Much of what Elizabeth David writes or recommends is at odds with advice in other books, but you can rely on her totally as long as you follow her instructions to the letter. A wonderful book to read even if you never ever bake.

The Best Bread Book, Patricia Jacobs, Harwood-Smart, 1975. An excellent book with basic and brand new recipes. Those not happy with the metric system will be pleased to see that the author puts imperial measurements first.

The Tassajara Bread Book,
Edward Espe Brown, Shambala
Press, Boulder, Colorado, USA,
1970, £2·40.
Although punctuated with a
good many liberated
Americanisms, this is something
of a cult book amongst devotees
of wholefood—rightly so, for
many of the recipes are both
innovative and delicious; the
two don't always go together.

Use Your Loaf, Ursel and
Derek Norman, Fontana, 1977,
£1·50.
Big illustrations and cartoon-
like instructions belie the serious
approach and excellent recipes.

Home Baked, George and
Cecilia Scurfield, Faber, 1956,
£2·00.
This small book is highly
regarded for its simple
presentation and interesting
basic recipes.

**Breads You Wouldn't
Believe,** Anne Lerner, Chilton
Book Company, Radnor,
Pennsylvania, USA, 1974, £1·50.
Another American combination
of good ideas and breathless
wonder at the world and those
who find themselves in it.

The Blessings of Bread,
Adrian Bailey, Paddington
Press, 1975, £6·95.
This is a lovely book to look at
and rather fun to read. But it
could trap the unwary. For some
reason the yeast proportions are
in 'packets'—American packets !
American yeast comes in $\frac{1}{4}$-oz
packs, equivalent to $\frac{1}{2}$ oz fresh
yeast, whereas English yeast is
usually packed in $\frac{1}{2}$-oz sachets,
equivalent to 1 oz fresh yeast.

The Complete Bread Book,
Lorna Walker and Joyce
Hughes, Hamlyn, 1977, £4·95.
A wide range of recipes,
attractively presented.

Leaflets
The Flour Advisory Bureau, 21
Arlington Street, London W1
(01-493 2521) publishes a
wide range of recipes and other
literature on the subject, suitable
for domestic, educational and
commercial use.

Measure-ments

Both metric and imperial
quantities are given in this book.
Use either the metric or the
imperial: never mix them.
    The current conversion
system is not mathematically
correct, e.g. 4 oz can officially be
either 100 g or 125 g—a
fluctuation of an ounce if you
take that to be 25 g. This book
has been consistent as possible
within this difficult situation.

Solid measure

grams	ounces
15	$\frac{1}{2}$
25	1
50	2
100	4
125	4
225	8
350	12
450	16
500	16-18
1 kg	32-36

Liquid measure

ml	fl oz
25	1
50	2
150	$\frac{1}{4}$ pint
250	$\frac{1}{2}$ pint
275	$\frac{1}{2}$ pint
400	$\frac{3}{4}$ pint
425	$\frac{3}{4}$ pint
550	pint
575	pint
1 litre	35 fl oz

Glossary

Additives: chemicals or
synthetic vitamins used in
commercial bread-making to
improve the performance and
keeping qualities of flour and/or
dough. See charts on pp. 86-7.
Aeration: synonymous with
leavening, *q.v.*
Aleurone: fifth layer of skin of
wheat grain, containing
protein, fat and minerals.
Ascorbic acid: Vitamin C,
used to speed up the leavening
of certain types of dough—see
pp. 86-7.
Baking powder: a mixture of
alkaline baking soda and one of
several other acidic chemicals.
When in contact with a liquid,
the chemicals produce carbonic
gas, which aerates any mixture
in which they are present.
Baking soda: bicarbonate of
soda. Only aerates dough in the
presence of an acid, e.g. sour
milk, buttermilk or a suitable
acidic chemical.
Bleaching: the process by
which the naturally creamy
endosperm (flour) turns white.
With time this happens
naturally, but today it is speeded
chemically.
Bloomer: a long, fat, rounded
loaf with flattish ends, diagonal
cuts; not baked in a tin.

Bran: the first five outer layers
of the skin of the wheat grain;
rich in minerals, bran is essential
roughage.

Cob/coburg: general name for any round loaf, sometimes slashed or pricked; not baked in a tin.

Cottage loaf: one made of two rounds of dough of uneven size, the smaller sitting on top of the larger.

Danish loaf: an oval, crusty loaf with a centre cut; not baked in a tin.

Endosperm: the major part of the wheat grain, consisting mainly of starch cells and granules.

Extraction: an indication of what percentage of the whole grain is present in a flour; for example, in 85% extraction flour, 15% of the coarse bran has been sifted out.

Farmhouse loaf: white loaf with 'Farmhouse' imprinted on the side; baked in a tin, and both wider and shallower than normal tin loaves, *q.v.*

Fermentation: another term for the growth (and subsequent side effects) of yeast; this term is usually used for brewing and wine-making rather than bread.

Flour: the result of grinding wheat or any other grain.

Soft flour is made from wheat grains with a limited ability to form gluten and is therefore unsuited to yeast cooking.

Strong flour is made from grains capable of producing much gluten, which is essential for yeast cooking.

French bread/sticks: white dough shaped into long rolls. As the French use only soft flour that absorbs little water and contains no bleach or additives, it is impossible to get the genuine French flavour using anything but French flour.

Germ: the embryo wheat plant in one wheat grain, very rich in vitamins (especially E).

Gluten: a substance formed by the protein in flour when it is moistened. Its elastic qualities enable it to trap gas formed by yeast or chemical aeration.

Leaven/leavening: a generic term for aerating or raising agents—yeast, baking powder and so on.

Roller mills: the most common means of making flour today. The grains are crushed and the various components (bran, endosperm, etc.) are gradually separated by a series of steel rollers.

Sandwich loaf: bread baked in an enclosed tin so that it has a regular square shape.

Soda bread: dough aerated with bicarbonate of soda and sour milk or buttermilk. Dough aerated with baking powder is commonly called soda bread, too.

Stone-ground: describes any flour ground in the traditional way, milled between two granite stones. The result can only be wholemeal flour but this may be sifted to produce other types of flour.

Tin loaf: term for all loaves baked in tins or pans. The basic tin loaf is long, oblong, with a high rise; if there is a central slash it is a 'split tin'.

Wholemeal/wholewheat: when used to describe flour, these terms indicate that nothing has been removed from the grain. UK regulations also prohibit anything being added to such flour. When used to describe bread, the terms indicate that only this type of flour has been used, but the dough may contain additives. See chart, pp. 86.

Wheatmeal: a term once used widely to describe the extraction flours, e.g. 81% or 85% flours, in which the figure indicates the percentage of the wheat grain included. 'Wheatmeal' is being phased out of commercial usage, and the extraction rate is now indicated on the packet instead. Some millers now call wheatmeal flour 'farmhouse'.

Yeast: common name for any fungi of the *Saccharomycetes* family, all of which feed on natural sugars and produce alcohol and carbon dioxide as by-products.

Index

Numbers in italics indicate captions

Additives, 92; dough, 86; flour, 85, 87
Afghanistan bread, 24
Ale barm, 21
Aleurone, 12, 13, 92
All-in method of bread-making, 31
Alum, 7
Anglicans, 9
Armenian chapati-type bread, 24
Ascorbic acid, 87, 92

Bagels, *56*, 58-9
Baguette, *28*
Bakeries, 25, *25*, 27, 28
Baking bread, 39 ·
Baking powder, 21, 23, 92
Baking soda, 21, 22-3, 92
'Balady', 25
Baptists, 9
Barley, 4, 6, 14
Barley bread, 7, 14, 56
Bath buns, 76
Beer breads, 60
Berliner kranzküchen, *72*, 80
Bleaching, 20, 26, 92
Blinis, 14
Bloomer loaves, *28*, 35, 92
Boston brown bread, 47, *48*
Bran, 12, 13, 19, 20, 27, 85, 92
Bread: dough, 9, *28*; additives in, 86; all-in-method, 31; deep-freezing, 90; faults in, 89; filling tins, 34; kneading, 32-3; leavening, 21-3, *22*; -making, 30-31, *31*; punching down, 34; refrigerating, 89-90; slapping down, 34; sponge method, 31; whole grains in, 54-5
Breaking bread, 8
Brioches, 66-7; frankfurter, 67; sausage in, 66-7
Buckwheat, 14, 43, 55
Buckwheat cakes, 14, 55

Burke, Edmund, 11

Chapati, 24, *24*, 42
Cheat's sour-dough, 46
Chebbakia, *72*, 74-5
Cheese breads, 60
Chelsea buns, *72*, 76-7
Chemical raising, 22-3, 26-7
Chollah, 58
Christian Church, 8-9
Cob, 37, 93
Coburg, 37, 93
Coconut coffee twist, 75
Cold storage, 89-90
Cooling and storing, 40
Corn bread, 48
Corn meal, 14, 55; hushpuppies, 56
Cottage loaf, 37, 93
Country oat bread, 48
Courbet, Gustave, *13*
Cranach, Lucas, *4*
Creole rice cakes, 80
'Les Cribleuses de Blé' (Courbet), *13*
Crisp breads, *17*
Croissants, 62; jambons, 67
Crossing bread, 6
Crown loaf, 37
Crusaders' bread, 43
Crusty loaves, 39-40
Cuts and slashes, 34, 53

Daisy loaf, 37
Dampers, 44
Danish loaves, 35, 93
Danish open sandwiches, 83
Danish pastries, 63
Danish pastry shapes, 64-5
Deep-freezing, 40, 90
Diet breads, 85
Doughnuts, jam, *72*-3
Dutch rye, 44

Egyptian bread-making, 4
Ember and ash bread, 48
Endosperm, *12*, 13, 18, 19-20, 93
Enriched breads, 58-9
Exercise bread, 44
Extraction flours, 20, 93

Fancy breads, *40*
Farmhouse flour, 20
Farmhouse loaves, *28*, 35, 93
Faults in finished loaves, 89

Fermentation, 93
Flour, 93; additives to, 85, 87; adulteration of, 7; buckwheat, 55; composition, 88; corn meal, 14, 55; extraction, 20; malted grains, 55; milling, 18-20, *18-20*; rice, 55; rye, 55; stone-ground, 18, *19*; white, 12, 13, 20, 26, 28, 30; wholemeal, 13, 20, 28, 30
French bread, 25-6, 35, 53; baguette, *28*; chandelier of, *27*; sour-dough starter for, 45
French-style stick bread, 53, *56*, 93
Fresh fruit loaf, 60
Fruited and spiced bread, 59-60

German bread shapes, *28*
Glazing, 39
Gluten, 12, 15, 19, *28*, 93
Good health bread, 58
Goul, Philip, *10*
Graeco-Roman bread-making, 4
Granary bread, 55
Greek bread: Easter, *9*; sesame, 54
Griouches, *72*, 74
Gugelhopf, 79

Hand-mixed, hand-shaped breads, 24-5
Hawkshead cake, 75
'Hot bread' shops, 27

Jewish bread, *9*; bagels, *56*, 58-9; chollah, 58; religious laws concerning, 8, 9
Jewish Sabbath meal, *9*
Jordan loaf, 51
Juvenal, 11

Kentucky apple bread, 59-60
Khachapuri, *56*, 70-1
Kneading, 32-3, 34
Knot, 36; Staffordshire, 36

Lardy cake, 78
'The Last Supper' (Goul), *10*
Lattice shape, 37
Leavening, 21-3, 93; chemical raising, 22-3; equivalents, 87; salt-raised breads, 23; sour-dough breads, 23; wholemeal bread, 85; yeast-, 21-2

Lincoln, Abraham, 11
Liquid, in bread-making, 30-31
Literature, concept of bread in, 11

Loaf tins, 30; filling, 34
Loaves: baking, 39; cooling and storing, 40; crusty, 39-40; faults in, 89; glazing, 39; shaping and decorating, 34-8; testing, 39
London bakers' guild, 8
Loukoumades, 72
Lutherans, 9

Malted grains, 55
Marie Antoinette, 11
Masa harina, 25, 42-3
Mass-produced bread, 27-8, *28*
Mass, use of bread in the, 6, 8-9
Middle-of-the-road bread, 51
Millet, 14-15
Milling of flour, *18*, 18-19, *19*; roller, 19-20; stone-ground flours, 19
Moreland Close crunchy cake, 76

New System of Domestic Cookery, A, 7
No-knead loaf, 50

Oat bread, 7, 15; country, 48
Oat flakes, 15
Oatmeal bread, 56
Oats, 6, 15
Oktoberfest, Munich, *28*
Oliebollen, 72
Omar Khayyám, 11
Ovens, 26; pizza, *68*; at Pompeii, *6*; Welsh clay, *7*; wood fire burning in, 7

Pahlava, 71, *72*
Pancakes, 14
Paratha, 42
Passover, 8, 9
Pastries and brioches, *61* 62-7
'The Payment' (Cranach), *4*
Perfect party loaf, 82-3
Petits pains au chocolat, 67
Pissaladière, 68
Pitta, 25, 54, *56*; stuffed, *56*
Pizza, 68
Pizza oven, *68*
Plaits, plaiting, 38; chollah, 58;

as decorations, 38; savoury wholemeal, *56*; sweet white, *56*

Polish babke or baba, 79
Pompeii, bakery at, *6*
Pooris, 42
Poppy-seed loaf, *72*, 78-9
Poppy-seed rolls, *28*
Potato bread, *23*, 56
Potato sour-dough starter, 45
Potato water, in bread-making, 31
Prairie bread, 48, *48*
Pretzels, *28*
Protestants, 9
Punching down, 34

Raisin and malt loaf, 59
Refrigeration, 40; of bread, 90; of dough, 89-90; of yeast, 89
Religious theory and practice, bread in, 8-9
Rice, 15
Rice bread, 55
Rice cakes, Creole, 80
Rice flour, 55
Rising times, guide to, 86
Roller milling, 19-20, 26, 93
Roll shapes, 36
Roman Catholic Church, 6, 9
Romans, 4, 6, 11
Rosette, 36-7
Roughage, 13
Rum babas, 72
Rye, 6, 15, *17*; Swedish crisps, 43
Rye bread, 15, *17*, 23, 56; Dutch, 44; sour-dough, 46, *48*
Rye flour, 55

Sally Lunn, 77
Salt, 30
Salt-raised breads, 21, 23
Sandwich loaf, 93
Sandwiches, 81-3; Danish open, 83; pinwheel, 81; silhouette, 81; tea, 82; toasted, 82
Santorini, winnowing on, *26*
Saracen wheat flour, 14, 43, 55
Sardinian 'paper' bread, 24
Savarin, 71
Savoury breads, 60
Scriptures, bread in the, 10-11
Semolina ghoriba, 73

Shakespeare, William, 11
Shamrock, 37
Shaping and decorating loaves, 34-8
Sifting or bolting, 19
Slapping down, 34
Sliced loaves, 26-7
Slimming breads, 85
Soda breads, 22-3, *23*, 47, 93; Boston brown bread, 47, *48*; wholemeal, 47, *48*
Sour-dough breads, 21, 23, 44-6, cheat's, 46; French, 45; rye, 46, *48*; wholemeal, 45
Sour-dough starters, 45, *46*; potato, 45; yeasted, 45
Sour or yeasty flavour, 89
Soya, soya flour, 15, 31
Spirals and swirls, 36
Split-tin loaf, 35
Sponge method of bread-making, 31
Staling, 89
Standen loaf, 55
Stone-ground flours, *18*, 19, *20*, 24, 28, 93
Swedish rusks, 70
Swedish rye crisps, 43

Tacos, 43, *48*; filled, 43
Testing bread, 39
Texture of bread: close, heavy, 89; uneven, with holes, 89
Thomas, Dylan, 11
Tin loaf, 93
Tortillas, 24-5, 42-3, *48*; filled, 43
Turkish hand mill, *20*
Twain, Mark, 11
Twist, 36; knotted, 36

Unleavened bread, 8, 9, 42-4

Vienna loaf, 35, 58

Watermills, 8, 18, 19
Welsh clay oven, 7
Wheat, 4, 6, 12-13, *13*, 26, 55; grain, *12*; international production and trade, *16-17*; soft, 12; strong, 12; Turkey red, 12
Wheatgerm, *12*, 13, 19, 20, 85, 93; bread, 56
Wheatmeal flour, 20, 93
Wheatsheaf, *40*

White breads, 6, 7, 8, *8*, 52-4,
  85; basic, 52; French stick,
  53; Greek sesame, 54;
  middle-of-the-road, 51;
  pitta, 54; sliced loaves, 26-7;
  short-time, 52
White flour, 12, 13, 20, 26, 28,
  30; bleaching, 20;
  composition, 88; plain, 12
Whole grains, 54-5
Wholemeal breads, 7, 8, 24,
  50-1, 85; flowerpot, *56*;

Jordan loaf, 51; leavening,
  85; pitta, 54; no-knead loaf,
  50; savoury, with ham and
  olives, *56*; soda bread, 47, *48*;
  sour-dough, 45; used as
  trenchers, 8, *8*
Wholemeal flour, 13, 20, 28, 30,
  40, 93; composition, 88;
  stone-ground, 19
Wholewheat flour, 20, 93
Windmills, 8, 18-19, *19*
Winnowing, *13, 26*

Yachtsman's bread, 70
Yeast, yeast-leavening, 19, *21*,
  21-2, 25, 26, 27, *28*, 30, 31,
  85, 93; compressed, 21, 22;
  deep-freezing, 90; dried, 22,
  30; international cookery
  based on, 68-80;
  refrigerating, 89
Yeasted breads, 50-60
Yeasted sour-dough starter, 45

Credits

Artists
Vanessa Luff
Ilric Shetland
Max Ansell, Temple Art Agency
Anne Isseyegh

Photographs
Adespoton, 29
Bodleian Library, 8
Barry Bullough, 41, 49, 57, 61,
  73
Danish Food Centre, London,
  84

Mary Evans Picture Library, 23
The Flour Advisory Bureau, 22
Richard and Sally Greenhill, 27
Sonia Halliday, 10, 20
Long Ashton Research Station,
  University of Bristol/Dr
  Robert Davenport, 21
Mansell Collection, 18
Margaret Murray, 24, 26
Musées Nationaux, France, 13
Nationalmuseum, Stockholm, 5
National Museum of Wales/
  Welsh Folk Museum, 7(b), 90
Radio Times Hulton Picture
  Library, 6
Ann Ronan Picture Library, 7(t),
  19

Ronald Sheridan, 9(b)
Shaun Skelly, 69
ZEFA, 9(t), 25, 28 (t and b)

The chart showing the
composition of flours on p. 88 is
reproduced by courtesy of the
Flour Advisory Bureau. The
author wishes to thank the
Jordan family, the Flour
Advisory Bureau and the
International Wheat Council
for their helpfulness in providing
information.

Cover
Photograph: Barry Bullough